STARTING UP & SCALING UP A

BUSINESS

ANDREW CHRISTOPHERS

Matador
Unit E2 Airfield Business Park,
Harrison Road, Market Harborough,
Leicestershire. LE16 7UL
Tel: 0116 2792299
Email: books@troubador.co.uk
Web: www.troubador.co.uk/matador
Twitter: @matadorbooks

ISBN 978 1803136 301

British Library Cataloguing in Publication Data.
A catalogue record for this book is available from the British Library.

Printed and bound by CPI Group (UK) Ltd, Croydon, CR0 4YY
Typeset in 12pt Avenir Next by Troubador Publishing Ltd, Leicester, UK

Matador is an imprint of Troubador Publishing Ltd

To

Theo, Rachel, Helen,

Jack, Mia, Will

and Arabella –

my positive and

human-first influences.

INTRODUCTION

"Culture eats strategy for breakfast."[1]

25 years ago, three of us started a small marketing agency. We remained small for many years. But there was something special and unique about the business. Special enough for one person to say recently, "Working at Brand Genetics was one of the best decisions of my life."

More than 90% of start-ups fail within ten years.[2] But today, we are not only still going, we are bigger than we have ever been – and getting ever more so. Still not big, by many

[1] Management Consultant & Writer Peter Drucker
[2] TechRound.co.uk: Why Do Nine Out of Ten Startups Fail Within a Decade?

industry standards, but big enough to have achieved a £5m global status, employing over 30 people across 3 continents. We continue to help invent the future for some of the world's biggest brands, with major clients including ABInBev, Mondelez, PepsiCo, Reckitt and Unilever. And as importantly, the business has retained its unique and special character. Something we refer to as "human-first".

This is a book about Starting Up and Scaling Up. How do you start something from scratch, and then build a thriving and successful business? What lessons do you learn along the way, and what challenges do you face as you begin to grow? How do you manage the tension between the fluidity of a creative start-up and the structure and organisation that are then required to underpin it?

But above all else, this is a book about people. My belief in life is that we should all celebrate what people are great at – not beat them up for their deficiencies! I have always valued positive thinking: being able to empower, enable and encourage people to achieve their full potential – and not just in work, but in life too. I also believe that if you can create a strong and distinctive human culture in a business, then you can not only attract great talent, but you can retain and develop it too. And as you help people grow and progress themselves, so they help you grow and scale your business. It's a win-win situation!

So what does it mean "to be uniquely human"? How can you build a truly "human-first" business – an engaging culture, where people are empowered to do their best work, and to grow both personally as well as professionally? What are the principles that can help create a human-centred culture, where people feel valued, motivated and fulfilled? And how can you maintain and evolve the ethos and values that made you unique and successful in the first place?

In the following pages, I tell the story of the first 25 years of Brand Genetics, and how we have built a "human-first" insight and innovation consultancy. I have tried to capture some of the significant experiences using an A-to-Z structure, which highlights 26 different key learnings and challenges. Each themed chapter is brought to life with a series of real-life human stories and first-hand personal examples, all summarised into key take-outs.

My objective is to give insight and understanding to anyone who wants to know more about the realities of starting up and running a small business, and creating a work culture that puts people firmly at its heart. I also want to record 26 of the reasons that I think have made our business special – what makes Brand Genetics "Brand Genetics"?!

More personally, what compelled me to write this book? I think that one of the benefits of growing older is gaining a greater perspective – on life and on business too. I have certainly found this since my first grandchild was born: grandparenting is a very different experience from parenting! It's been the same with my work experience. When you're embroiled in the cut and thrust of running a small agency day-to-day, you can't always see the bigger picture or appreciate the significance.

I have always liked T. S. Eliot's line about this: "We had the experience but missed the meaning."[3]

So I want to share my perspective, and I also want to unpack what building a "human-first" business means in practice. Recently, a colleague said to me, "Andrew: you are the human heart and soul of Brand Genetics." That was very flattering, but am I? And what was meant by this comment?

I inherited many memorable quotes from one of my Co-Founders, Michael, as we built the business. One of these was, "All talk is self-talk." So I hope the following pages are not too full of "me". To help mitigate against this, it is undeniably true that anything we have achieved over 25 years at Brand Genetics has been a real team effort, and a shared journey. So my enduring thanks to the following list of colleagues (cast list in approximate order of appearance) who have all helped shape what Brand Genetics has become today.

---

[3] T. S. Eliot: *Four Quartets*

John Kearon

Michael Holgate

Paul Marsden

Mike Read

Patrick Tully

Hervé Hannequin

Alessandra Masoero

Daryl Weate

Bob Wagner

Nicole Brannan

Olly Wicken

Rachel Clare

Tom Rowley

Blue Martin

Neil Stammers

Tom Ellis

Cliff Fawcett

Coralie Castel

Liza Makarov

Camila Marcondes

Matt Michaud

Abigail Ireland

Amy Daroukakis

Olivia Galvin

Chiara Rampulla

Marc Edwards

Charlotte Melford

Amanda Ayoub

Alice Yessouroun

Joella Vera Bril

Ben Preston

Neha Ahmed

Clemmie Prendergast

Nathania Messer

Andrea Sinclair

Kate Evans

Jordan Smith

Liz Thompson

Monica Zymberg

Fiona Barnett

Mia Christophers

Brando Guerreri

Lesley Salem

Simon Hall

Shivani Nirula

Catherine King

Frankie O'Donohoe

Yoann Hui

Holly Moore

Julz Donald

Poli Pieratti

Hattie Camp

Ciaran Nilan

Oli Kriskinans

Luiza Cesario

Mike Woolston

Hannah Scarf

Cecile Hemming

Rob Jordan

Alex Whyte

Andrea Namirembe

Marina Machado

Rachel Warby

Joanne Cattermole

Georgia Massie-Taylor

Dani Cronin

Andrew Stauffer

Gray Seiler

Sophie Lyon

Adam Hendrick

plus Finn the dog

(and Panda and

Goose).

Plus also our many

fantastic partners

and hundreds of

supportive clients:

our valued sponsors!

TABLE OF CONTENTS

A is for Ascent of Man   14

B is for Bravery   18

C is for Comfortably Uncomfortable   22

D is for Don't Take The Piss   26

E is for Empathy   30

F is for Fun & Feelgood Fridays   34

G is for Good to Great   38

H is for Human-First   44

I is for Integrity   50

J is for JFDI   54

K is for Kindness   56

L is for Letting Go   60

M is for Mutant Marketing   66

N is for Never Stop   72

O is for Optimism   76

P is for People   80

Q is for Questioning   86

R is for Relationships   88

S is for Speed   92

T is for Team BG   96

U is for Uncertainty   102

V is for Values   108

W is for We   114

X is for X-Factor   118

Y is for You   122

Z is for Zero to One   126

A is for Ascent of Man

Look for journeys, not destinations.

What's in a name? We called ourselves Brand Genetics (BG) for a reason. We set up, way back in 1996, using the Darwinian algorithm of evolution as our inspiration. The American philosopher Daniel Dennett described Charles Darwin's theory of evolution as "the single best idea anyone has ever had." Praise indeed! So we boldly proclaimed, to anyone who would listen, "All Marketing is Darwinian." Every new start-up needs a large dollop of self-belief, plus a degree of madness too.

At the beginning, there were three of us. John came with a background in advertising planning, Michael had previously run an innovation agency, and I had been working in client-side marketing roles. We soon met Paul, an evolutionary psychologist, who was to prove pivotal in helping us embed behavioural science at the heart of our business. Paul preached the gospel of "BV-SR": blind variation followed by selective retention. His university lecturer used to state, "Evolution is a 2-step process. I repeat, evolution is a 2-step process!"

So we applied this thinking to brands. Innovation was about descent with modification. Every new product or service has a huge amount of continuity (or shared genes) with previous market iterations. But to stand out and survive in a competitive environment, it must also embrace an (often small) new variation as well. This could be as simple as Gillette adding a new blade to its razors, or Häagen-Dazs bringing fresh cream into ice cream, to create the next generation of luxury products.

Now while I don't mind a bit of theory, I find a picture can be worth a thousand words. So I have always liked the Ascent of Man image – or Ascent of Humans, as we should more accurately call it. For me, it is evolution in action, and it represents both progress and innovation – especially next-generation or new category (as opposed to just new product) innovation. Each new figure has evolved from its predecessor, showing both many similarities, but also a significant competitive advantage too. In the stone ages, if a human's fingers became more dexterous, so more effective at picking fruit from a tree, that trait would be bred into the gene pool as a positive new attribute. The only aspect this image fails to capture is all the blood on the floor – the millions of evolutions that failed to survive and thrive.

So if I could summarise Brand Genetics in just one image, it would be The Ascent of Man. Indeed, we used this thought in one of our very first Christmas cards, when we were just a six-person team. The Ascent of Man picture reminds us that building a business (just like managing a brand) is about evolution and constant re-invention. Michael would always advocate, "stay dissatisfied" – even if we were just looking for a lunch venue!

Charles Darwin articulated the importance of change and adaptability, and we had to ensure we were an innovation agency that innovates itself. As you build a business, change remains the one constant. I remember thinking at one point, when we had just made a new, senior appointment, "That's it, we have our team in place now: job done." How wrong could I have been? Things are always changing: new challenges, new events, new projects, new people, new ambitions.

Latterly, we liked to call ourselves "a start-up with 25 years' experience." That was so we never rested on our laurels, but continued to stay curious and inventive in our thinking, looking for continuous improvements while embracing the new and different. As we grew, The Ascent of Man picture was also a great reminder that we were moving from a small to a medium-sized business – out of childhood, through our teens and even into early adulthood, where new demands and challenges needed to be faced.

Businesses (and their employees too) should look for journeys, not destinations. And we should all give ourselves permission to enjoy the ride. That's where the experience and the learning come from, and how people can grow and develop themselves. It's summarised well by Edward Monkton's Zen Dog[4] cartoon.

ZEN DOG

He knows not where he's going
For the ocean will decide –
It's not the DESTINATION...
...It's the glory of THE RIDE

A is for Ascent of Man:

- Building a business requires constant evolution and ongoing re-invention
- Embrace adaptability, and even the smallest of competitive advantages
- Ensure you can enjoy the journey – the experiences and the learning

[4] © Edward Monkton

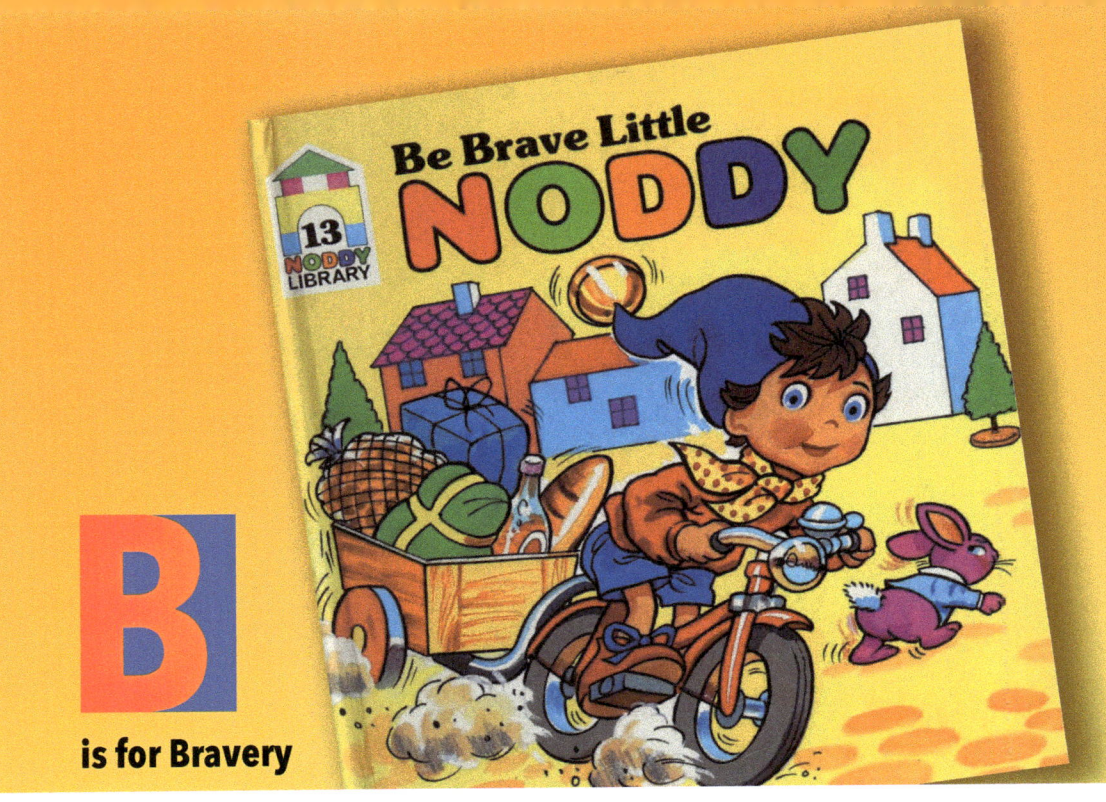

B

is for Bravery

Courage is not the absence of fear, but the triumph over it.[5]

When we first set up, our initial vision was "to perpetually disrupt the status quo". This was driven by John, who believed that 80% of any project should use new methodologies, and only 20% be known ones. It was certainly an ambitious aim, which meant we had to learn to embrace the unknown, and challenge the status quo. We took aim at conventional market research, labelling researchers as "innovation prevention officers". In the early days, we enjoyed this Will Rogers[6] quote: "If you're riding ahead of the herd, take a look back every now and then, to make sure it's still there!"

[5] Nelson Mandela
[6] Will Rogers, American Comedian & Actor
[7] *Only Fools and Horses*, British TV Sitcom

After John left, "Be brave, little Noddy" became Michael's own message to self. Michael was nothing if not, at times, a glorious contradiction. Sometimes he would worry we were adopting a "corner shop mentality" to building the business. Other times he would talk about "selling for millions!" We used to think we were like Del Boy and Rodney from Only Fools and Horses[7], "This time next year, we'll be millionaires!"

But once Tom joined us, having been MD at a previous agency, we changed gear in the bravery department. We made our first new senior hire for many years, with Cliff also joining us from Tom's old agency, Big Green Door. Cliff was planning to travel for a year, so it was only initially a six-month commitment for us. We joked that Cliff had resigned before he joined.

And as Tom began to get hold of the business, his bravery was awesome. I remember a project with Bacardi Travel Retail when Tom didn't want the client to feel he wasn't wholly committed to them. So, while he was working on a different project with another client in China, he still managed to conference call with Bacardi – at what must have been 2am in the morning – without them even knowing he was out of the UK! Foolish maybe, but certainly brave.

Once Tom and I bought Michael out, we signed up to sponsor the Global Innovation Forum. It was our first big 'bet', spending what was then serious money for us: something we would never previously have done. Tom, by now our CEO, was masterful in chairing the conference, with over 200 of the world's leading innovators in attendance – even when thrown by a fire alarm evacuation during the first keynote session. We still now chair this fantastic event, 10 years later. It brings together the industry's visionaries, disruptors, optimists and trouble-makers – the "crazy ones", as referenced in Steve Jobs' brilliant early Apple commercial, "Think Different".[8]

We were brave many years ago, when we accepted our first ever brief from Interbrew, the company that built into ABInBev, the world's biggest brewer. It was a brand naming brief for a new Belgian drink – and we had no brand naming experience. But we researched and learnt up some tools and techniques, and managed to deliver a successful workshop. It became the start of a highly successful relationship, which we kick-started further when helping them understand their identified need state areas, specifically the Social Catalyst space via a big global multi-market project.

I remember being quietly terrified when we signed our first 5-year office lease for our current Fitzroy Square London location. We were committing ourselves to c£0.5million, which seemed a massive bet and a significant amount of money. But we did it – and renewing the lease several years later was a much easier decision.

Tom was also brave and pragmatic with our geographical expansion. Camila, our super-talented Brazilian who had been our first ever intern, came to tell us that she wanted to return to

[8] Apple "Think Different" ad, narrated by Steve Jobs (1997)

her native Rio de Janeiro. While she had loved Brand Genetics, she said she would sadly have to leave us, after her six years in London. Tom instead asked her to head up our first ever overseas office, covering the LatAm region, where we were already developing significant global work. This became not only a great success but also a useful pilot for us, with so much of the learning helping us to launch a North American office several years later. It is also a great example of trusting your people and being open to giving new things a try.

When I first left the security of working client-side to help set up a start-up, I kept a quote from a Christmas card sent by my brother. It was kings riding camels, with the line, "Courage – to undertake the journey without knowing the destination." It felt very relevant to my own situation. I recently heard a similar sentiment expressed by England's new cricket captain, Ben Stokes, after winning his first four Test Matches while encouraging his team to play some daring and exciting cricket.

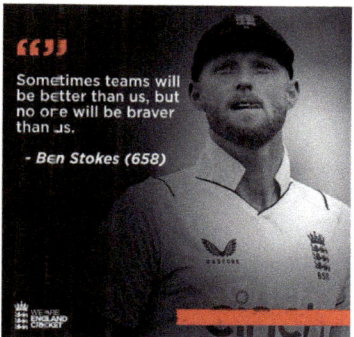

Sometimes teams will be better than us, but no one will be braver than us.

- *Ben Stokes (658)*

B is for Bravery:

- Embrace the unknown and challenge conventional thinking
- No risk, no reward – but don't confuse bravery with recklessness
- Trust your people and be open to giving new things a try

is for Comfortably Uncomfortable

Don't settle for the status quo: stay curious, remain restless.

The notion of being Comfortably Uncomfortable became a central part of our people and culture manifesto. The term was first used by Camila, who felt that every day since she first joined Brand Genetics, she had felt both challenged, but also supported too.

Being Comfortably Uncomfortable is finding the sweet spot between breaking new ground (so you are stretching and developing yourself, learning new skills) but also feeling supported by your colleagues and team, working in close collaboration. This helps promote a growth mindset and a culture of continuous improvement, where individuals can learn and grow, challenging themselves and pushing boundaries, while ensuring help is at hand when it's needed.

I remember one project in particular when Camila demonstrated these skills in abundance. We were running a challenging project for Britvic soft drinks in Brazil. It soon became apparent that the local market client, unsurprisingly, was much more comfortable and open when running sessions in Portuguese as opposed to English. This meant I could no longer run our series of planned workshops, and we needed to switch to Camila (as a local market speaker) leading all facilitation tasks; Portuguese with English simultaneous translation as opposed to the other way round. Camila rose to the task magnificently. The sessions were so successful that both clients and consumers alike ended up hugging her afterwards, in a typically Brazilian show of affection. I could only look on with admiration and pride!

In our experience, this notion helps promote a culture of continuous improvement, for individuals and for businesses too. Continual self-improvement and facing difficult new challenges are central to many successful sports teams too. The All Blacks[9] prize the New Zealand rugby shirt so highly that they believe players should "leave the jersey in a better place", and also be prepared to "plant trees you'll never see." Many of our Brand Genetics team have done just that.

C is for Comfortably Uncomfortable:

- Help people find their sweet spot, between breaking new ground but still feeling supported
- Promote curiosity and a growth mindset: a culture of continuous improvement
- Work to leave the business – and your people – in a better place than when they started

---

[9] *Legacy* by James Kerr

D

is for Don't Take The Piss

THE BG DTTP* GUIDE

Don't Take The Piss

CONTEXT

We strive to make BG an inspiring place to work:

A-team colleagues,
doing A-team work,
for A-team clients,
all within an A-team culture.

We work with some of the world's biggest brands, with global international travel opportunities. We have some flexibility regarding working times / locations, and a highly collaborative and supportive working environment.

We take real pride in helping our team grow and develop, giving them the right level of support and autonomy and encouraging them to follow their passions.

But within this multifaceted industry – and as we've grown – we've recognised that some 'guidelines' are necessary to help ensure clarity and consistency across the team. The aim is to help uphold our unique culture, and give some guidance on different elements of BG working life.

These "rules" are important, but perhaps more important are the two underlying principles – both rooted in our historical context – in which they are intended to be understood:

- Despite over 25 years' experience, we want to keep our ... which means giving our people auton... **the piss**" mind...

Trust your team, and create an adult-to-adult work environment.

At Brand Genetics we have always championed an adult-to-adult approach, empowering our people to self-manage and make their own decisions, without the need for approval or micro-management. Just as children like nothing more than to be treated as young adults – "give them roots, then give them wings"[10] is my favourite truth about parenting – so most self-driven professionals require much less hands-on management than many of us at first recognise.

For many years, we only had one company 'rule' or guiding principle: Don't Take The Piss (DTTP). This originated when

---

[10] Attributed to both Johann Wolfgang von Goethe and the Dalai Lama

we brought in our first two employees, way back in the days when mobile phone calls were astronomically expensive. On being presented with their new company phones, our new hires asked if they could use them to make personal calls. The dreaded thought of having to check through people's phone bills crossed our minds with horror. So we decided that any reasonable calls would of course be paid for by the company. But if you were phoning a friend in Australia every day, then maybe that wouldn't be covered by Brand Genetics. In other words, let's encourage self-regulation and promote an adult-adult mindset, not a parent-child one. And let's refer to this as the DTTP rule.

This guiding principle has continued to serve us well as we have grown. We have nearly always been rewarded when we have given people more autonomy and responsibility than we had first intended, and our team has grown accordingly, in both ability and motivation.

In the early days, Mars wanted one of us to join their internal innovation team, and all three of we founders were already busy. So one of our first employees, Patrick, who had joined from a client-side background, stood up for the task. Behind the scenes, we were worried about whether he could pull this off, and if he had sufficient experience and credibility: we wanted to set him up to succeed. But the trust and independence this gave him was the making of him as a consultant; he never looked back, and we never had cause to doubt his assured ability in future.

In later years, we gave Tom the space and remit to lead, run and build the business – and he was masterful at this. And our future Head of North America, Liz, really came into her own when Cliff was away on sabbatical. This enabled her to fully step in and step up to own a key client relationship, with ABInBev's ZX division. We tried to allow our people to be the best they could be, realising that young and ambitious employees relish nothing more than being trusted and given responsibility and autonomy. We aimed to build a business which was the very opposite of a 'command-control' company. And this really paid dividends when Covid struck. People were obviously forced to self-manage more than ever before – and the energy and dynamism of the team were awesome to behold.

As the company grew bigger, we continued to use our DTTP mantra, but we also realised that we needed a little more guidance and explanation for our growing team than just this one 'rule' alone. We therefore wrote the DTTP guidebook for all employees, covering everything from flexible working and time off in lieu to working late and business expenses.

Despite 25 years' experience, we wanted to keep our start-up mentality, which meant giving people autonomy, within an over-riding 'don't take the piss' mindset. This required us to trust everyone to be respectful, responsible and to use their own judgement. All 'rules' were guidelines and principles only, not specifics. Everyone is uniquely individual, so every individual case will be different. But if all people can be given the personal autonomy to think like owners, then they are much more likely to act like owners too. We were proudly independent as an agency, with our future in our own hands, so we wanted to encourage our people to adopt this mentality too. And just think of the management time that this can save!

Netflix advocate something similar in their iconic 2009 HR PowerPoint deck[11], which went viral with more than 20 million web viewings. Their expenses policy (in the Freedom and Responsibility section) was just five words long: "Act in Netflix's Best Interest". This is all that's needed, if you value freedom over control.

Personally, I loved the simplicity of the one DTTP rule. But I realised, once it was necessary to write the DTTP rulebook, that we were moving from start-up to scale-up. And all the new challenges that this would entail.

D is for Don't Take The Piss:

- Trust, autonomy and self-regulation, within an adult-to-adult work environment, will massively increase motivation and reduce management time

- Look for principles and guiding frameworks – don't try to manage the specifics

- If you encourage your people to think like owners, they are much more likely to act like owners too

---

[11] Netflix's "Freedom & Responsibility Culture" deck (2009), by Reed Hastings and Patty McCord

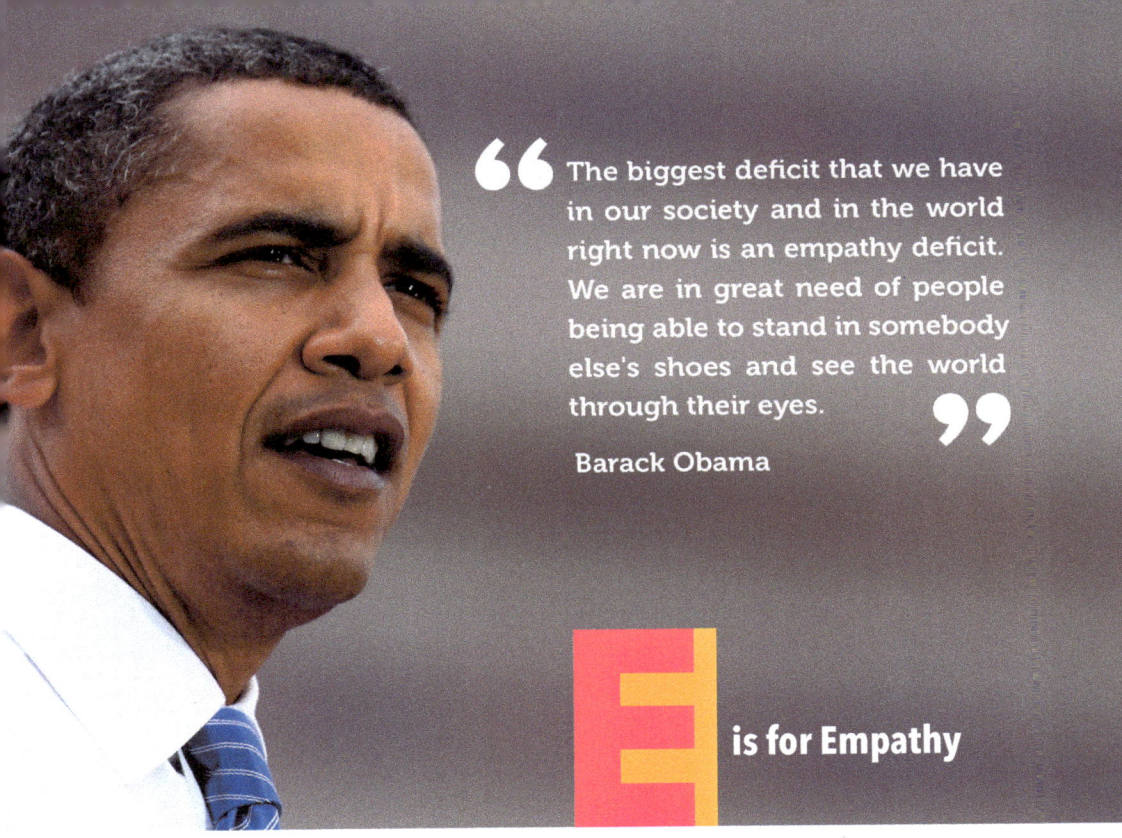

E is for Empathy

Walking a mile in someone else's shoes.

We realised that understanding human motivation, and indeed understanding one another, is primarily about having empathy. Abraham Lincoln once said, "I don't like that man; I must get to know him better." And a more recent American President, Barack Obama, says, "The biggest deficit we have in our society and in the world right now is an empathy deficit."

Empathy is a remarkable human capability. It is our ability to see and feel things from someone else's perspective. If we can step imaginatively into the shoes of another person, this can provide us with emotional insight into how it feels to be someone else.

Empathy became central and essential to us in understanding our own internal team, in building and developing client relationships, and also in developing new research techniques. To understand human motivations and behaviour, we have to be able to walk a mile in someone else's shoes – and also help our clients to walk in their customers' shoes too.

Paul authored an empathy playbook for this very purpose, titled *In Their Shoes*. It explains that while some people are naturally more empathic than others, empathy is a skill that can be trained and improved in us all. The marketing empathy deficit means that while 80% of brand executives believe their brand offers the best experience, only 8% of their consumers agree![12] So as innovation and research become increasingly dominated by quantitative data, analytics and algorithms, market researchers need empathy more than ever to see the humans behind the numbers.

[12] Bain & Company (2005): Closing The Delivery Gap

The playbook therefore outlines a series of practical empathy-based activities, promoting perspective-taking and emotional mirroring, using unscripted and observational techniques, to help you research and innovate better from a consumer perspective. The 'plays' generate emotional insight by helping you understand people's feelings and motivations. They are taken from the worlds of psychology, design, therapy, medicine and investigative journalism, where empathy-based research has long been used for insight generation.

One of the most powerful examples of empathy research I ever experienced first-hand was in a nightclub in São Paulo. We were tasked with understanding how beer could better infiltrate into the heartland of spirits in clubs. We had previously talked about the psychology of social 'mirroring', when one person subconsciously imitates the gestures, behaviours, or attitudes of another. And our young female research respondent elicited exactly this response, when a young male approached her on the dancefloor. A 30-second film of this 'courtship' became a central part of the subsequent research debrief, explaining motivations, behaviours and requirements in the nightclub setting.

We found that empathy worked hand-in-glove with experimentation in our market research techniques. For innovation, we have long been champions of consumer co-creation – mixing clients and consumers in creative workshops, where group 'energy' and non-verbal communication are so critical. We are also big fans of embracing start-up thinking, ensuring a lean approach to innovation: test and learn, product placement, and preto-typing, to name but a few. And it is the combination of these two facets – empathy and experimentation – that ladders up to truly human-first propositions and new creative opportunities.

Recent industry research[13] has shown that understanding and empathetic leadership can be more important to employees than salary. To feel valued, people want to feel understood. And for this, it's so important to try to recognise that everyone's not wired just like you. Diversity must be understood, as well as embraced. Humility in leadership is vitally important for this.

One final thought on empathy. During the global pandemic, it became even more important that we could understand one another. So the most important question to ask everyone became not just "how are you?", but "how are you… really?"

E is for Empathy:

- Emotional insight comes from stepping imaginatively into the shoes of someone else, to see and feel things from their perspective
- Empathy and experimentation can get beneath surface findings and data to uncover new creative opportunities
- Empathetic and understanding leadership can be more important to people than salary

---

[13] Forbes (Sept 2021): Empathy Is The Most Important Leadership Skill

is for Fun & Feelgood Fridays

You don't have to be serious to solve serious issues.

Laughter is the social glue that brings and holds us all together. Laughter pre-dates language, and we know that it increases creativity and reduces stress. Teams that laugh together achieve more, and laughter can be a key measure of a happy workplace and a buoyant company culture.

Working in a client service consultancy can be brutal and stressful on occasions. Big problems to tackle, multiple priorities, short turnaround times. My heart always used to sink when a client came in with an urgent brief, declaring "time's really ticking on this one."

But shared camaraderie can make the seemingly impossible not only possible but enjoyable too. We came to recognise that, although we were about understanding how the human mind works, what we do isn't brain surgery! So our guiding principle was to enjoy the work, and to help others enjoy it too, celebrating the successes, both big and small. We would always have a few drinks at the end of the week, but we also believed that fun wasn't just for Feelgood Fridays. (In fact, with less Friday office presence post-Covid, fun was for Thirsty Thursdays and even Two-Tin Tuesdays as well!)

Inventing the future for some of the world's biggest brands should be a fun and exciting challenge. But at times, things could of course go wrong. I remember one particularly dominant and challenging client deciding (halfway through a workshop) that we were adding no value at all, and he could do a better job himself. It's never worth challenging someone like this directly in a public forum, so I let him take the flipchart pen, and run the rest of the session himself. We got the project back on track, moving the agenda back within our control, and into one of our tried and trusted methodologies. This delivered some stunningly successful co-creation sessions in Italy, with the lead client slapping himself on the back for delivering such great work!

To help us keep things in perspective, we adopted a phrase, "No one's ever died from a broken workshop." It served us well. Although, on one occasion, we came alarmingly close.

A German moderator was in full flow, but adamant that his junior assistant should open the window, midway through a consumer research workshop in a 12th floor office building in Hamburg. Keen to do the right thing, his assistant leant right out, over a centre-pivot window, losing his balance in the process. We clawed him back to safety, to much relief and hilarity.

The tone of a business is set from the top. Tom never takes himself too seriously, and this can be contagious. In business (as in life) you have to learn to laugh at yourself. We instigated an "HR Jar" at Brand Genetics, into which any funny or vaguely inappropriate comments were captured on Post-It notes. This generated some memorable quiz moments at company socials and Christmas parties: which quote is attributable to who? And always sitting proudly, blu-tacked to the top of the HR Jar, was a plastic model of St Jude, the patron saint of lost causes. This was donated by an Irish client with a wicked sense of humour, when he briefed us to help revitalise their ambient soup brand.

I recall many memorable moments from across the years, including leaving some workshop output on a train, and having to blame an "over-zealous cleaner" in my client explanation. And when we won our first ever project in the US, innovating a new Cadillac car for General Motors for the new Millennium, Michael was super excited to be traveling business class. He wanted to make the most of the airport lounge's hospitality, embracing the full-on experience. When his flight was called, he felt he still had time for an extra plate of olives. He then said he "didn't want to be seen to be breaking into an unseemly trot" – and proceeded to miss the flight!

I also remember a desserts project for Müller when we invented a "speed dating" innovation tool. If one person was "crumble" they had 30-seconds to get together with "trifle" to see what new dessert they might create. My sister (then a solicitor with a top London firm) could not believe that I was being paid to speed date puddings! I guess the important lesson is we should all maintain a healthy sense of perspective about our work.

F is for Fun & Feelgood Fridays:

- Laughter is the social glue of a happy workplace and a buoyant company culture, so enjoy your work and keep things in perspective
- Celebrate and enjoy the successes and the funny moments as well
- You can be serious about your work, but you don't have to take yourself too seriously

G is for...

Strive for excellence, not perfection.

Cultivating a growth mindset is vitally important for any business that wants to attract and retain top talent. Initially this was driven by our own organic growth, and by giving real autonomy and responsibility to what was then a small team, so they could really learn and deliver. But as we grew, we not only needed more process and structure around the business, we also had more of a responsibility to grow and develop our people too.

We used the *Good to Great*[14] book as a guiding light for some

---

[14] *Good to Great* by Jim Collins

of this work, and it helped us adopt a mindset of constant improvement, never being satisfied with the status quo. We always felt we earned our fees in the final 5% of any project: the first 95% might be more of a given, so we really had to crank up the thinking to deliver true delight in the final outcomes. So many companies are data-rich but insight-poor. Or as the old saying goes, "If only Unilever krew what Unilever knew."

A helpful lens could be moving through the 'What?" (the main research findings) to the "So What?" (the impact and meaning of these) and finally into the "What Now?" (the implications and resultant actions). We weren't delivering the final 5% unless or until we got to the "What Now?" We also found it was much more productive to go into market research with working hypotheses and insights, to ensure we could get further, faster and deeper.

Cliff was a master of delivering outstanding work, with his creative planning brain. Obsession was admirable, and indeed sometimes necessary, but we realised there was an important distinction between perfection and excellence – and we had to strive for the latter, not the former. Mia (who joined us with a thorough background in research) teamed up with Cliff to drive our Project Excellence initiative. They became our internal guardians of standards and expectations, including gaining objective client feedback after every project. By positively seeking feedback and acting on it, we were able to keep refining and improving our client deliverables. They both also authored an essential internal guide, the "BG Way", which outlines the key signature actions and behaviours that underpin all our work.

I remember an interesting conversation with the founder of Flamingo, a one-time highly successful competitive agency. She said they built their business on the reputation of their work alone, with every debrief becoming a calling card for the next piece of work. As such, they only needed a very minimal focus on new business in their early growth years.

At BG, Liz was a real inspiration and role model for self-improvement, embodying our desire to help deliver ongoing growth and development for our people, and for our business too. She always wanted to focus on areas where she could learn and improve, and (after 360-degree peer reviews) she would ask for extra detail on all the (non-attributable) 'negative' feedback from the team. She recognised her strengths and where to lean in, but was always more motivated to better understand her gaps and areas to improve. She delivered highly impressive live webinars across the globe, but always in advance asked us to listen out and let her know what she could do better next time.

When we hit our targets in 2019, the biggest ever year in the company's history at that point, we took the team away to San Sebastián to celebrate. We got everyone out and back in Q1 2020 just before the global lockdowns struck! We themed this as a 'Good to Great' trip, using the time together to define our greatness – what makes us special and different, what is our internal uniqueness, and how does this manifest itself externally to our clients?

We also focused this thinking on each individual as well, recognising that what makes 'you' great is what makes 'us' great too. Everyone completed a user manual 'superheroes' task, articulating their own special 'superpower'. We came back from San Sebastián with, amongst others, The Inquisitor, Captain Positive and Pressure-Man! And also with the soundtracks to accompany these characters – what music tracks make you feel great when you get up onto the dancefloor?!

The Good to Great mindset was important in recruitment too. It's often so difficult to make decisions on people, especially when you hardly know them. But I recently heard a great tip on this, which is that you should only ever have two responses post interview. It's either a "Hell Yes" or a "No".

Marketing consultancy can become a very precise and even up-its-own-backside discipline! After the action focus of 15 years client-side, I found the adjustment was, at first, both daunting and draining too. On my first day in our new Brand Genetics start-up, I spent over three hours with John and Michael crafting just one sentence, the objective statement for a new Britvic packaging brief – one of our first ever projects. We re-expressed and challenged our own thinking and articulations so often that I wondered whether I was cut out for this industry after all. But it's that rigour that is so often required – to move from Good to Great. And when we finally solved that particular brief, it resulted in the launch of a new brand from Robinsons called Fruit Shoot. All the angst had not been in vain!

G is for Good to Great:

- Adopt a growth mindset, for your business and your people – look for constant and ongoing improvement
- Obsession is admirable, and internal standards must be upheld – but strive for excellence, not perfection
- Recognise within your team that what makes each individual great is what makes your overall company great too

H is for Human-First

66 Human-First means... Helping people – colleagues, consumers, clients – achieve their goals and realise their full potential 99

Technologies change, businesses change, markets change – the one constant is human nature.

It took us almost 20 years to articulate our "human-first" positioning. But thereafter, everything became so much clearer and easier. It acted as our North Star to govern our work and thinking, including our new product offers. It dictated our relationship-building with partners and clients. And it also defined our behaviour, culture and recruitment. This acts as a case study on the importance of a business defining what it stands for, plus how and why it is different from its competitors. Never an easy process, but certainly one worth persevering with.

When we first started, we were driven by disruption, and a new approach to innovation (see M is for Mutant Marketing). So our early strapline was "The awesome creative power of evolution." We were inspired by Darwin's theory of evolution, and we were going to unleash this awesome creativity into new brands and marketing. We even took this theme into our annual Christmas cards.

We then came to focus more on the theories that underpinned our insight and innovation practices. We had always been rooted in psychology and behavioural science, so we evolved to talk about "Applying evolutionary science to marketing." This was true, but maybe not especially compelling.

The next iteration of our positioning was when we challenged ourselves to think about what benefit we were actually delivering for our clients. We articulated this as "Forward thinking, future edge." This worked for us, positioning us clearly in the front-end insight and innovation space. But was it sufficiently distinctive or ownable?

We finally sat around in a room, discussing big data, automation, AI and robotic developments, and Paul volunteered the thought "The future is human." This resonated deeply with us all, and gave us a very ownable thought on which to anchor our future business development. The link back to Darwin's genetic theories was inherent, and made more contemporary by understanding people's individual characteristics, represented by the human DNA. The thought also encapsulated our expertise and passion for understanding human motivations and behaviours. So we evolved quickly through "Creating positive human futures" and "Human-centred insight & innovation" before we landed on "Unlocking growth by thinking human-first."

"Human-first" stood up to scrutiny, and soon became a powerful encapsulation of all that we do. We found the "human-first" mantra was universal. Whether customers, consumers, users, clients or colleagues, people are always humans first. It was unifying. What unites us is stronger than what divides us, and the truths that unite people across different cultures are the strongest foundations on which to build global brands that resonate at a deeply human level. And it was also constant. Human nature, the inherited psychological and behavioural traits embedded in our DNA, remains consistent and unchanging over time. So while technologies, businesses and markets may all change, the one constant is human nature. So by understanding this, we could help our clients build relevant and enduring brand propositions.

Internally, "human-first" governs how we think about our people at Brand Genetics. We care about the work, but even more importantly, we care about our people. So "human-first" became a great shorthand, governing our behaviour and ensuring we looked out for one another, treating everyone as "humans" not "employees". This included championing personal development, celebrating diversity, and balancing work and wellbeing.

Externally, it ensured we strove to understand deep-rooted human behaviour, zooming out to see the wider context of people's lives through our market research, viewing all respondents as "humans" not "consumers". It ensured we rooted our work in real human needs, and we valued human relationships (getting to know the person behind the client), as we helped them build meaningful, positive brands.

So we defined "human-first" as "helping people achieve their goals and realise their full potential." Those "people" could be colleagues, consumers or clients. We wanted to understand the motivations of all these audiences, to help them achieve a positive impact and positive growth too.

"Human-first" became the anchor around which we were able to develop both our Mission and our Vision.

OUR MISSION

WE DRIVE BETTER BUSINESS DECISIONS THROUGH A DEEPER UNDERSTANDING OF WHAT MAKES PEOPLE TICK AND BRANDS GROW

OUR VISION

TO INSPIRE EVERY BUSINESS WITH A HUMAN-FIRST FUTURE

"Human-first" also began to influence our thinking about future research methodologies, ensuring they were designed to look at brands in the context of people's lives, not vice versa. We therefore championed more immersive and experiential approaches, to deliver more real insight and understanding. These included Conversations in Context (instead of focus groups) and Consumer Closeness programmes, to get to work where real meaning and motivation resides. In practice, this means hangouts in bars, supermarket shop-a-longs, and ethnographic delving into kitchen cupboards. And it also means working collaboratively with clients via live debrief sessions, to capture the 'killer thoughts' and key learnings.

It was our task to do some of the clever stuff, using psychological frameworks and behavioural science, but as importantly it was our role to align people's hearts and minds, and to facilitate the team's thinking onto the same page. Never underestimate the power of getting people into the same room, to align different agendas and points of view. A simple 'Hopes & Fears' task is a great way of facilitating this.

The human-first move also required us to challenge and change our company logo. What had served us well since the start, the Brand Genetics bar code, was now beginning to look too much like a 'product' focused icon and was therefore insufficiently 'human'.

Some inspired design work[15] helped us evolve into a Brand Genetics DNA, which maintained a link to our past, but heralded a much more 'human-first' future!

H is for Human-First:

- Define what you stand for as a business – what makes you different and compelling – and everything else becomes so much clearer and easier

- Human-first is universal, unifying and constant – whether customers, consumers, users, clients or colleagues, people are always humans first

- A human-first approach can help people achieve their goals and realise their full potential

---

[15] www.cathyheng.com

is for Integrity

Share the glory, share the pain.

Honesty and transparency should lie at the heart of any successful small business. People look to the leaders, and the values of any business are set from the top. Sir Alex Ferguson echoes this in his book *Leading*[16], concluding that the one most important word for leading is 'consistency'. The integrity with which a business is led will always be visible, whether you are aware of it or not, and it will contribute massively to long-term employee engagement: is this a business that I trust and want to be part of, or not?

---

[16] *Leading* by Sir Alex Ferguson

We believed in a "share the glory, share the pain" mantra, so people knew exactly where they stood. This was with respect to business and financial performance, which was of course especially important in the more challenging times, as during the Covid pandemic. We were open about how we were doing, using adult-to-adult communication, which helped empower the team to take responsibility. If you're fully aware of a situation, you are much more likely to help find solutions to resolve it. So it was gratifying, as we emerged from the pandemic, to be able to pay everyone in the business a £1k Covid 'bonus', for helping us through those difficult months.

We always tried to be fair with our people, and with our profits too. In the very early days, we had the idealistic notion that all salaries would be equal: one pay grade fits all. We tried this for a year or so, but soon realised that it wasn't fair. The business owners were rightly and inevitably shouldering higher degrees of responsibility – and we didn't want the rest of the team to have to be worrying about new business every evening and weekend either.

But we did keep hold of the principle that, while we wouldn't of course publish everyone's salary, we should be able to look anyone straight in the eye and justify why they were being paid what they were, versus anyone else, should we ever need to. We tried to pay competitively, and liked to push through pay rises before people asked for them – although we didn't always achieve this.

We adopted a set formula for paying out company profits, based around three key 'pots' – one was for staff bonuses, one was for shareholder dividends, and one was retained profits to invest back into the business, to fund further growth. This served us really well for 20-plus years, enabling us to be fair with our people and their remuneration, while also preventing an annual debate about what to do with the money. We also opened up an 'internal market' for share ownership, enabling senior team members to buy into the business. Again, this was with set formulas around share values each year, allowing complete transparency about the costs and also the benefits involved. The more share owners we had in the business, the more we were genuinely able to "share the glory".

Integrity demands being honest with one another. We tried to embrace honest feedback and used the excellent book *Radical Candor*[17] to help with this. In it, Kim Scott tells a memorable story about a complete stranger intervening to discipline her wayward young dog at a busy New York traffic crossing. "SIT!" the stranger bellows at the dog, who miraculously obeys him. Kim cannot believe what she has just seen. The stranger continues, "I can see you love your dog very much, but I can also see you'll get him killed. Please realise, I am not being mean to your dog, just clear." This conversation changed Kim Scott's life. She came to advocate the power of "radical candor" – caring personally, but challenging directly. She says that a great boss excels in "saying what you really think, but in a way that still lets people know you care."

Feedback and candid conversations in the moment are so important. Don't save these for annual or six-monthly reviews. You would never discipline a child in six months' time, and any sports coach would pass on feedback in the moment, so it can have an immediate benefit.

We sometimes found it difficult to hold people accountable in our positive and human-first environment. In truth, we probably practised "empathic candor" more than the "radical" version. But it was vital. Just as with Kim Scott's dog, we had to be honest and truthful in how we communicated with our people. We needed to find more discipline and drive greater accountability as we grew. But these things are so much easier if they're done with real integrity.

I is for Integrity:

- The integrity with which a business is led will always be visible, whether you are aware of it or not
- Honesty, transparency and accountability will help empower and motivate your team
- Feedback should be given in the moment – directly but in a caring way

---

[17] *Radical Candor* by Kim Scott

is for JFDI

No decision is a bad decision, but no decision is a bad decision.

In my client-side days, I recall a member of my team who couldn't decide whether to go on a decision-making course. I empathised with her. Making decisions is never easy. But indecision and analysis paralysis are much more dangerous.

In the early days of Brand Genetics, we had so many ideas and options – new methodologies, new theories, new positionings for the company. We found it very difficult to be selective or to choose and close things down. But without making clear decisions, we were unable to put the power down on anything.

I once read that the best managers don't make better decisions, they just make more decisions. This rings very true with my Brand Genetics experience. We were at our best when we were decisive. That's when we got s*it done, we gained traction and we learned from it. And the converse was also true. That's when we lost momentum, drive ard focus, and when we frustrated both our people and ourselves.

Tom coined a useful phrase, "wet cement", for when we were working in the pre-decision or interim stages. You often need this thinking and creative time, to explore options and challenge one another's thinking. The important thing is then to recognise when the cement has to harden.

Finally, I had thought that JFDI was an Australian phrase. But I understand it's a common IT software development term, used to describe a request, generally from a manager to a developer. It obviously stands for Just F**king Do It, although it's also rather quaintly claimed to mean Just Focus and Do It.

J is for JFDI:

- Without making clear decisions, you won't put the power down on anything

- Indecision leads to analysis paralysis, frustration and loss of momentum

- Be clear about when you're in creative development mode, but also when you need to move from debate to decision and action

"What do you want to be when you grow up?"

"Kind" said the boy

K is for Kindness

Kindness cannot be given away... because people give it you back.[18]

We recognised our duty of care to our people, and set out to build a company with a good heart. We cared about our work, often passionately, but more importantly we cared about one another too. And our care extended beyond our direct employees, to our associates, our partners and our clients too.

[18] Steve Black, Sports & Business Coach

When we needed to start setting targets, to help us plan and manage our growth, we were keen to think of "team as well as targets", and "people alongside profit". We wanted to balance work and wellbeing for our people.

Before Andrea joined us, as our HR & Office Manager, she said she wanted to find a company with a good heart. She had previously worked at a similar style company, so she knew what she was looking for. And of course, it takes one to know one. She brought with her an innate sixth sense, which made her a trusted confidante for our people. She was someone they could turn to, catching up on an ongoing basis to air frustrations and difficulties, whether professional or personal, all in the strictest confidence. What also impressed me was how younger people and newer recruits responded to this. Oli, a great champion of mental health and wellbeing, and someone mature way beyond his years, asked us (soon after joining) who cares for the carer? He wanted to know, was Andrea OK?

When Ben, our new business manager, unfortunately had his flat burgled, he was particularly upset to have a 'multitool' stolen – one of his go-to DIY tools, with sentimental value attached too. This loss couldn't be undone, but it was truly heartening to see the team spontaneously hold a whip-round to buy him a replacement.

Kindness should extend to showing courtesy and understanding, even if and when people move on and leave.

I felt it was as important how somebody felt about Brand Genetics when they left the company as it was when they first joined. And we often therefore encouraged new hires (including Tom before he joined) to speak to our "ex's", to get a true picture of what the company and its people were really like. This helped build a strong "alumni" effect, which I think can be the hallmark of a successful and vibrant company culture. On moving on from Brand Genetics, Frankie (one of our Associate Directors) was generous enough to say, in her leaving speech, that she had never come across a company with as much kindness as Brand Genetics.

Monica joined us from Unilever in Brazil, and was an all-action bundle of energy, positivity and proactivity. She was a brilliant team member, but after less than a year she felt the pull again of re-joining a big business. I was (secretly) devastated. But of course we had to accept and indeed respect her decision. It was probably right for her, even if it was disappointing for us. She stayed in contact, and wrote to us a couple of years after leaving. "I have now been outside for longer than I was actually part of the BG team, and I can genuinely say that I can hardly notice. BG was, and is, much more than a workplace for me. You gave me opportunities and trusted me unconditionally. You were my partners in crime and supported every decision I made, including the hardest one, when it was time to go. That's true leadership, and more than that... it's being human, and caring for each other beyond any business objective."

I love the simplicity and truthfulness of Charlie Mackesy's philosophy of life. None more so than the line, in his book *The Boy, The Mole, The Fox and The Horse*[19], when the Mole asks the Boy, "What do you want to be when you grow up? Kind, said the boy." We keep this picture up in the BG office.

K is for Kindness:

- Set out to build a company with a good heart, caring about the work, but more importantly caring about one another
- Look at team as well as targets, people alongside profit, and to balance work and wellbeing
- It's as important how somebody feels about a company when they leave as it is when they first join

---

[19] *The Boy, The Mole, The Fox and The Horse* © Charlie Mackesy

L is for Letting Go

Moving from hands-on to hands-off.

As a founder, it is very hard to let go and delegate when you are building a business. But you will never truly succeed, nor achieve any sustainable scale, unless or until you can do this.

Delegation is very tough for start-ups, because you often relish doing everything yourself at the beginning. Coming out of corporate life to set up Brand Genetics, I was used to having a PA, a Head of IT and an Office Maintenance person, not to mention a team of marketers. But in my new start-up world, I truly enjoyed the responsibility of the buck stopping firmly with me. In big corporate client marketing departments, it can be easy to hide behind other people. But in a new start-up, doing a good job is all about you. Success means winning projects, delivering delight, and getting re-hired. The alternative is that you earn no income!

When we founded Brand Genetics, the internet was in its infancy and email was only just beginning to emerge. So after every idea generation session at a client workshop, we would have to write up and then print out a catalocue of ideas. It was then off to the post office, to weigh up and send off the output – asking each client to fax back their lead ideas! But I took a perverse pleasure in doing all this myself. Later on, when we got our first office, it was (literally) the founders' job to change the lightbulbs. Also to buy the milk and tea bags, to fix the printer and internet, and to put locks on the windows.

The All Blacks[20] famously have a "sweep the sheds" mantra, where top class rugby internationals are never too big or too important to duck their duties of cleaning out the changing rooms after matches. The same is true in SME's (small to medium-sized enterprises), where the Chairman or CEO should never be too self-important or detached to make the tea or change the ink cartridges. "Never be too big to do the small things"[21] is a great philosophy for managing people.

But initially, in the early days, we made the mistake of believing that our work could only be delivered by seniors and highly experienced individuals. The work was, we felt, difficult and challenging: we saw ourselves as "the SAS of Insight & Innovation".

[20] *Legacy* by James Kerr
[21] Eddie Howe, Newcastle United FC Head Coach

But to grow and develop, and of course to empower and motivate others as well, you must let go a bit. You have to get yourselves working 'on' rather than 'in' the business, ensuring you don't get too lost in the 'weeds'.

Michael used to tell a good story about this, which he had picked up from a sales manager during his days at GSK. A manager is running a fleet of 15 different milkmen, and one of them calls in sick one morning. What should the manager do? His first instinct is to jump into a milk float himself, and complete the delivery round for his sick colleague. But this will mean there are now 15 milkmen, and no manager. It's therefore the wrong decision. He should hold back, and keep managing the others.

Delegation is about trusting your people. How can you lead if you don't trust others? It would mean that every decision is down to you, and you alone. Sir Alex Ferguson shares three great lessons about delegation in his book *Leading*[22]:

1. Don't try to do it all yourself. Fergie stood back from taking training sessions and found he could then see much more. It also gave his assistant a clear role. Working through others is the difference between leadership and management. We all need to hire the right people, and then get out of the way to allow them to execute the talent we first saw in them.

---

[22] *Legacy* by Sir Alex Ferguson

2. Listen to people younger than you. They are the future and are at the cutting edge. We should always be prepared to listen and learn. In our business, we soon recognised that the younger team members were often much more aligned with our clients' target audiences than we may have been. When Ben first joined us as an intern, he said that not one day went by when he wasn't asked for his opinion. In reality, he was the target age for so many of our beer-related projects, so of course we wanted to know what he thought. (And he wasn't shy in telling us, either!)

3. Explain to the people around you that you care about little details – but that it's their job to attend to them. The great leader is unafraid of delegating authority, and refrains from micro-management. Sometimes this is easier said than done, but maybe the Covid-enforced lockdowns helped us all trust more and micro-manage less.

Delegation became easier when we developed more processes. As we began to grow, so many of our problems and challenges fell into the "growing pains" bucket. Start-ups are typically not very good (at least at first) at structures and organisation. It's all much more fluid and organic to begin with. But we needed plans and processes the more we grew, whether on project excellence, resourcing, project and new business tracking, 5-year plans, recruitment or career development. We also needed a clearer structure, to drive autonomy and delegate decision making. We implemented three 'pillars', with a different Director heading up each of Projects, People and Performance. We also empowered the more junior team members, assigning direct responsibility for areas such as Diversity & Inclusion and Sustainability.

Letting go, ultimately, became about more than just empowering other people. As I grew older, I wanted to step back – but I found it extremely difficult to do so. I guess 25 years of living, sleeping and breathing something isn't easy just to give up. Before he stepped back, Michael used to say he didn't want to feel like a onetime prize-fighter, stepping back into the boxing ring for one last fight, and leaving beaten and demoralised. For me it was about wanting to leave the party while I was still enjoying it and the music was still playing, not waiting for the lights to come on at the end!

It was hard to let go and contemplate leaving my own business. Another business founder told me recently that starting her own business was easy, running it was really hard work, but leaving it was nigh on impossible! I was helped by hearing about something called Founder's Syndrome, a recognition that your skillset might be better suited to starting up than scaling up. I could empathise with this sentiment as we continued to grow, and it enabled me to feel more positive about my changing role. I could work fewer hours because we had built a successful and inspiring business and recruited a great team of people. I now had to trust them to build on this, with their own talent, energy and ambition.

An ex-client (who worked with us during his spells at Bacardi, Russian Standard and Jägermeister) asked if I was like Young Mr Grace in the old *Are You Being Served* TV series[23]. He is wheeled out every few months, and tells everyone, "Carry on – you're all doing very well!" That, I told him, is exactly what I'm like!

L is for Letting Go:

- You will never achieve sustainable scale unless you delegate to your team, moving to work 'on' rather than just 'in' the business – don't try to do it all yourself!

- Listen and learn from people younger than you: they are the future

- Recognise the different skillsets and requirements of scaling up as versus starting up

---

[23] *Are You Being Served?* British TV Sitcom

is for Mutant Marketing

Mutations are the source of all progress.

Brand Genetics' first ever product was the Mutant Marketing Programme. Having set up shop as a new and disruptive innovation agency, we were asked to run a day's brainstorm by Spillers Petfoods (later acquired by Nestlé), who became our first ever client. They wanted to spend £2k, but we managed to upsell them into a six-week programme costing c£35k. We would always present our costing page with the line, "As you can see, we are practically a registered charity!"

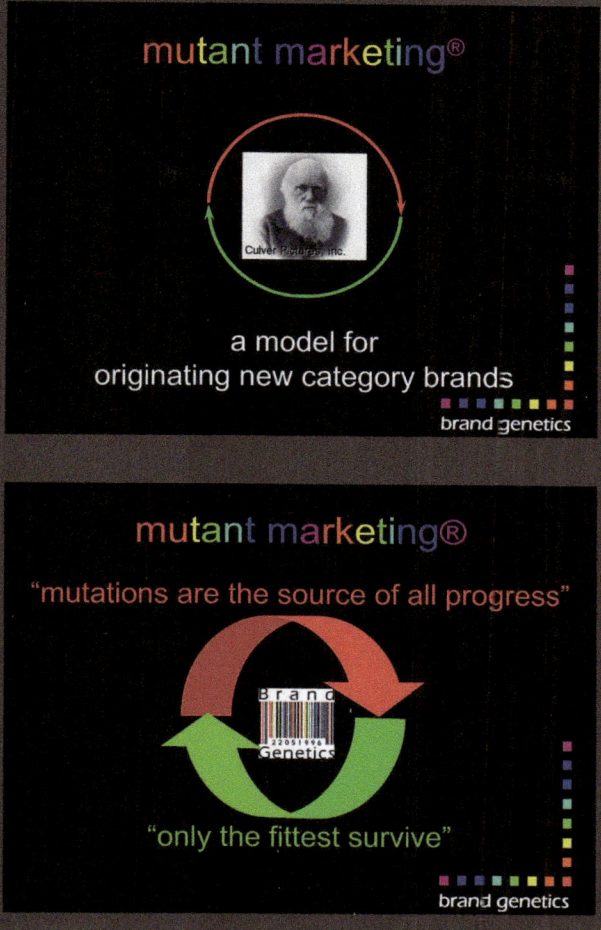

The Mutant Marketing Programme (or MMP) was based on the Darwinian algorithm that "Mutations are the source of all progress" but that "Only the fittest survive." This provided us with a distinctive and memorable mode for creating new brand life, or the "creds to die for" as we used to call our credentials deck; (notwithstanding the early garish PowerPoint charts!) John wrote a provocative article titled "Innovation at a Crossroads: Is Marketing Killing Innovation," and we had this published in the Marketing Society's Market Leader magazine, in their Autumn 1999 edition.

This all helped establish Brand Genetics as a new and different business. And it attracted a string of big new clients in the early days – both the visionary and the desperate! The tools and techniques we subsequently developed can be traced back to those early days. But, in the best traditions of evolutionary science, they evolved and developed via a 'test and learn' mindset. We did, at least, practice what we preached.

Our original vision was to help clients invent new categories, not just new products. This goal – which today would be termed disruptive innovation – was rooted in our early 'mutant' thinking. We challenged convention by creating large catalogues of 100+ new category mutations. In what is now called product-led innovation, we used the genuinely creative tools from Systematic Inventive Thinking[24] to generate form before function ideas, only subsequently looking for market fit. We had a raft of innovation stories to support our thinking, including 3M using a glue that wouldn't stick to invent Post-It notes, and Two Dogs[25] inventing alcopops, when an Australian fruit grower had too many lemons, so he experimented with brewing them to create the world's first alcoholic lemonade.

The MMP also included a highly creative but brutal team selection day, to whittle down the lead candidates, using advocacy and counter-advocacy techniques, fusing mathematics with passion. This was followed by detailed concept manifestation, which we called a Brand-DNA process, to make all new ideas real. I remember Michael once challenging a client relentlessly when she wanted "something for the gin & tonic moment". Gin & tonic already exists, so she had an objective, but not an idea. "Make it real" became our rallying cry – and we would try to make prototypes of new products too, to help invent the future.

We then co-created with both Pioneer and Conservative consumers (people with high or low change orientation bias), using high-energy and highly interactive big group workshops, to contrast a glimpse of the future with the resistance of the present. Today, Pioneers would be called early adopters or opinion leaders, and our iterative "only the fittest survive" approach would be labelled "test & learn" or "co-creation".

Much of what was cutting-edge then is now widely advocated today. Disruptive innovation is here to stay; product or design-led innovation is increasingly fashionable; many have recognised that early adopters hold the key to innovation success; and The Lean Startup[26] has popularised the minimal viable product (MVP) 'test and learn' approach.

But the MMP put us on the map, it differentiated us, and ensured we stood for something memorable. At the time, a fellow marketer rather pompously told us, "Would the CEO of Diageo want a mutant? I think not!" And an early client at Yellow Pages listened patiently to John and Michael deliver our story before commenting, "You're two space cadets, awash

[24] Systematic Inventive Thinking: www.sitsite.com

[25] Two Dogs Ready-to-Drink alcoholic beverage, first launched in Australia in 1993

[26] The Lean Startup by Eric Ries

on a sea of gobbledegook!"

But that was the point – to challenge conventional thinking. And within our first two years, we had run MMP's for a host of well-known clients, including American Express, Elida Faberge, General Motors, Lever Brothers, Pedigree Masterfoods, Sara Lee, UDV and United Biscuits. And alongside some real 'mutant' ideas (such as Rotten Apple cider and solid 'dry' Pocket Scotch) we had also helped Britvic create Fruit Shoot, using the push-pull sports cap pack to give street cred to kids, while giving mums the reassurance of the Robinsons brand name.

We encouraged our clients to embrace the uncomfortable and the unusual and to be more ambitious with their innovation. Michael said, "Nobody ever got fired for not launching a Perrier." We found that conventional research will over-reward the familiar and punish the new. Our Pioneer Panels methodology therefore became a compelling new way to address this challenge of how to test future-focused ideas.

But while many of our principles remain the same, today's innovators face new challenges and require new solutions, so we continue to break new ground. Despite now being an established business, tackling global projects for major corporates, we maintain our start-up mentality, with a willingness to challenge innovation inertia. It's this inherent dissatisfaction with the status quo that still motivates and inspires us today. We continue to work at the future's edge, delivering forward thinking insight and innovation, to help keep our clients ahead of the game.

M is for Mutant Marketing:

- A genuinely new approach is required to create a new and different business – be distinctive and memorable, and challenge conventional thinking

- Adopt a 'test and learn' mindset

- Maintain a start-up mentality – an inherent dissatisfaction with the status quo – to keep challenging innovation inertia

N is for Never Stop

The more I practice, the luckier I get.[27]

Starting a new business becomes an obsession. A bit like former England rugby union player Jonny Wilkinson relentlessly practising his penalty kicks, I sometimes wonder whether start-up founders need to be slightly unhinged. It's certainly not for the faint-hearted.

Setting up and running a business is a 24/7 occupation. It becomes all you ever think about, morning, noon and night.

---

27 Attributed to both golfers Arnold Palmer and Gary Player

It's therefore vital to find some kindred spirits, to help share the burden and spread the load.

A lot of the work is relentless and thankless too. But you have to put in the hard yards, overcoming obstacles and roadblocks, in order to succeed. I saw it as being like "cake" as opposed to "icing". The vast majority of the work is hard graft or "cake"; you can only occasionally stop to enjoy the accolades or "icing". This analogy helped explain to me why one of our senior hires didn't quite work out. He was more focused on the "icing" than the "cake"!

James Dyson talks compellingly about obsession and never stopping, reminding us of the value of failure too: "I made 5,127 prototypes of my vacuum before I got it right. There were 5,126 failures. But I learned from each one. That's how I came up with a solution. So I don't mind failure."

We adopted a "never stop selling" mantra, soon after Tom joined. This was because we recognised that whenever we got busy (as a small team) we were taken out with delivering the current project work. We would then fail to line up the next new job, and a period of downtime would inevitably follow. To level out this "feast or famine" cycle, we had to hold our nerve, and keep on selling new work, even when we had little capacity to deliver it. And we found that success breeds success. Just as clients seem to be able to detect if you're under-utilised and desperate to win new work, so they seem able to sense when you're busy and in demand – and that's when you become most attractive to them: they want a share of the action!

We developed a range of successful selling tools alongside stimulating content. "Trends that Count" was a cleverly named forward-thinking piece, and "Co-Creation that Works" helped us sell this other new methodology. Tom put together an inspired set of BRIC market insight summaries, which at a stroke positioned us as having global reach and expertise, across Brazil, Russia, India and China – and beyond. And Marc, with his new business drive, subsequently took these activities to new levels, structuring annual content into ongoing campaigns.

As the team grew, we adopted another "never stop" mantra – "never stop recruiting". We found it was much harder to play catch-up: we didn't have the time to find great people when we were already under-staffed. It also became harder to induct, train and integrate them when everyone was already fully stretched. So we had to speculate a bit to accumulate. And talent is such a precious thing. If we found the right candidate, we would endeavour to hire them, even if the need was less immediately apparent. We were always on the look-out for the next fantastic new BG-er!

As we began transforming our business growth, I remember a taxi ride with Tom in New York. We were en route from JFK airport to Manhattan, to run a project for Reckitt. It was one of those journeys when we both felt we had made a real breakthrough. We listed five key success factors for building Brand Genetics – and a "never stop" came in at number two:

1. Bravery

2. Never stop selling

3. Deliver great work

4. Focus on what we stand for (what benefit do we deliver to our clients?)

5. Free ourselves up to work on (not just in) the business

As I say, we added "never stop recruiting" to this list at a later date. But the reality of starting up and scaling up a small business is that you "never stop obsessing". You never switch off, and in reality, you never stop worrying either.

N is for Never Stop:

- Starting up a new business is an all-consuming obsession
- It's vital to find some kindred spirits, to help share the burden and spread the load
- Never stop selling, and never stop recruiting either

is for Optimism

Optimism is a happiness magnet. If you stay positive, good things and good people will be drawn to you.[28]

Positivity can go a long way in building and shaping a business, as it can in life too. It's always easy to think of barriers and problems, but where are the opportunities and solutions? We adopted the attitude that the pint was always "half full".

We had a "pillar of positivity" in the office, onto which we would record and post client feedback and positive

---

28 American gymnast Mary Lou Retton

testimonies. It became a great way of celebrating our successes, and some clients who had visited the office even made it a personal objective to feature on the "pillar"!

Optimism was not just a state of mind, but a company purpose too. We came to champion the mindset of positive thinking to create a positive environment, and we practised 'positive innovation' to drive 'positive growth'. We defined this as growth with a positive purpose that adds sustainable business value: new products and services that make people's lives better and more enjoyable, via more simple or intuitive solutions, ideally ones that have a positive impact on the planet too. Positive growth was an understanding that the world doesn't need "more stuff" right now, but rather "better stuff". We wanted our thinking and brand recommendations to help people live happier, healthier and more fulfilled lives.

This tied in with our focus on understanding human motivations, since that could help us deliver more purposeful solutions. The key to finding lasting growth and impact was getting beyond human behaviour to understand people's instincts and core motivations – reaching beyond what they say and think, to how they feel, and why they feel that way. This could unlock not just positivity, but human happiness and wellbeing too. We even produced a pack of Positive Innovation cards, distilling a wealth of scientific and academic literature in psychology and design to identify 18 validated insights to help develop innovation that drives true human happiness.

These include areas such as the ARC of Human Happiness –
which shows that our happiness can be determined by our
Autonomy, Relatedness or Competence in any given situation.

Positivity can be contagious. Leading is about having a
goal and a vision, but it also about how you act, inspire and
encourage. Sir Alex Ferguson[29] says leaders should "help
others believe they can do things they didn't think they were
capable of. Make others understand that the impossible
is possible." This, he concludes, is the difference between
leadership and management, counselling that the two most
powerful words in the English language are "well done!"

Positive affirmation is so important, in business and also in
life. Steven Bartlett[30] encourages us to do this: "If you think
something nice about someone, please tell them. This is the
easiest way to add positivity to a world that desperately needs

[29] *Legacy* by Sir Alex Ferguson
[30] British businessman & entrepreneur Steven Bartlett on LinkedIn

it." As long as you are authentic and you mear it, then there is nothing more uplifting than calling out your positive thoughts about and to your colleagues.

So there is something both rewarding and motivating about the power of positive thinking – and in innovating for human happiness, to create more positive human futures.

O is for Optimism:

- Never underestimate the value of positive encouragement and affirmation
- It's often easy to see barriers and problems, but look beyond them to find opportunities and solutions
- Positive thinking and innovation can drive true human happiness and wellbeing

P is for People

People who are smart, with heart, and a touch of self-start.

If estate agents talk about Location, Location, Location, then for building a business, it is all about People, People, People. Without great people, you don't have a business – especially if you're a small creative consultancy. So many companies talk about people being their biggest asset, but do they really act that way?

When we first started, our vision was to work with A-Team People doing A-Team Work for A-Team Clients. We deliberately listed these in that order, because A-Team People were (and still are) the most important. We spend so much of our daily lives with our work colleagues, so they should be inspiring and exciting people. The A-Team Work followed, because we wanted our people to help invent the future for big global clients – inspiring and exciting people need inspiring and exciting work! And the A-Team Clients both because we wanted to work on leading iconic brands, but also because somebody has to pay for it all!

Over the subsequent years, we had many attempts at trying to define what we meant by A-Team People. At first, we talked about whether people had an inherent 'Ready Brek glow'[31] to them: would you want to sit next to them at a dinner party? We then raised the stakes to think, would you go on holiday with them? This was never, of course, a literal question or requirement, but it was a good shorthand – not least because our work could involve long-haul flights and a week away working intensely with a colleague on another continent. So would you be happy sitting on a plane with someone for 10 hours? And when you and they are back in the office, would they fit in well on the 'middle table' in our open plan office, where many of the more vocal team members would often choose to sit?

After Fiona joined, she rather wonderfully said, "I have found my people." And as an ex-advertising planner, she was also able to articulate what she meant by this. She felt that Brand Genetics people were "smart with heart". Our team was full of bright and capable people, certainly, but they also looked out for one another and really cared – about their colleagues

---

[31] Ready Brek UK advert (1976): "Central Heating for Kids"

as well as their work. We were often asked at interview, what makes someone successful at the company? We realised it was the go-get or self-start people who really enjoyed and thrived in our at-times fluid and unstructured environment (partly the consequence of working in any ad-hoc or project-based consultancy). Indeed, we found that many of our successful hires had previously or currently started something up themselves or had a 'side hustle', fuelled by their own personal drive and entrepreneurial spirit. So we reached a better articulation of what makes a Brand Genetics person: it is someone who is "smart, with heart, and also a touch of self-start."

So that's what we tried to find, recruit and retain – talented people, with human values who can provide their own drive and motivation. People with the unique combination of smart, heart and self-start. A nice example of the BG entrepreneurial spirit in action was when we moved into our Fitzroy Square offices, and a couple of the team decided they wanted us to set up a bar, to help fuel the Feelgood Friday feeling. We couldn't then afford neon lights, so they bought plastic lighting instead, and fixed up a DIY board: "Bar Genetics" was soon open for business!

The late, great Sir Bobby Robson, ex Newcastle and England football manager, said, "Sign good people, not just good players." Rafael Nadal, arguably the greatest tennis player of all time, says, "I'd rather be remembered as a good person than as a good player." And the New Zealand rugby philosophy is also that "better people make better All Blacks,"[32] with their pithy team-building mantra being "no dickheads". In business, as in sport, no individual is ever bigger than the team.

Most of our hires, I am pleased to report, were highly successful. But just like with new product concepts, you often learn as much from those that fail as those that succeed. Of the people who didn't work out for us, there were usually some common themes, which we became able to look out for. These included a lack of self-drive or self-motivation, a requirement for more structure than we were able to provide, a more 'hawkish' mindset (in a company of 'doves'), or a lack of trust, honesty or integrity.

The other thing I learned was to treat people as people – and whole human beings – not as employees. At first, whenever anyone left or was thinking about moving on, I hated it and would take it too personally. But I came to recognise that not only is this often what the individual needs in their own life, but it can also benefit the business. New people bring new ideas, new energy and new opportunities, to help build, challenge and develop high-performance teams.

---

[32] *Legacy* by James Kerr

I also realised that sometimes you can 'keep' people by 'letting them go'. Cliff went on a couple of travel sabbaticals, returning both times with renewed ideas, passion and commitment. And Paul always valued having independence outside Brand Genetics, over the years combining his own academic career with his BG consulting, and working anywhere from Miami to Luxembourg, Brighton to Antigua. I think this is the responsible, progressive and enlightened way to manage people in future. Just like with flexible or hybrid working – let them choose, not you.

As we grew, people and people management took up an ever-growing proportion of our time, which could on occasions become emotionally draining. But that is natural, and something that should be cherished, embraced and prioritised. It's just far too important not to.

To conclude on people, I was always struck by Tim's speech in *The Office*[33] about working life and your colleagues: "The people you work with are people you were just thrown together with. You don't know them, it wasn't your choice, and yet you spend more time with them than you do your friends or your family. But probably all you've got in common is the fact that you walk around on the same bit of carpet for eight hours a day." Brand Genetics was different. Colleagues were more than just colleagues. We shared values, ambitions, hopes and fears. And I think this is what makes a business unique,

---

[33] Ricky Gervais: British TV sitcom *The Office*

attractive and compelling. The people, and more importantly their human connection to one another.

> **P is for People:**
>
> - Try to define a blueprint for the type of person who will thrive in your company
> - Hire good people, not just good professionals – no individual is bigger than the team
> - Treat people as people – whole human beings, not just employees

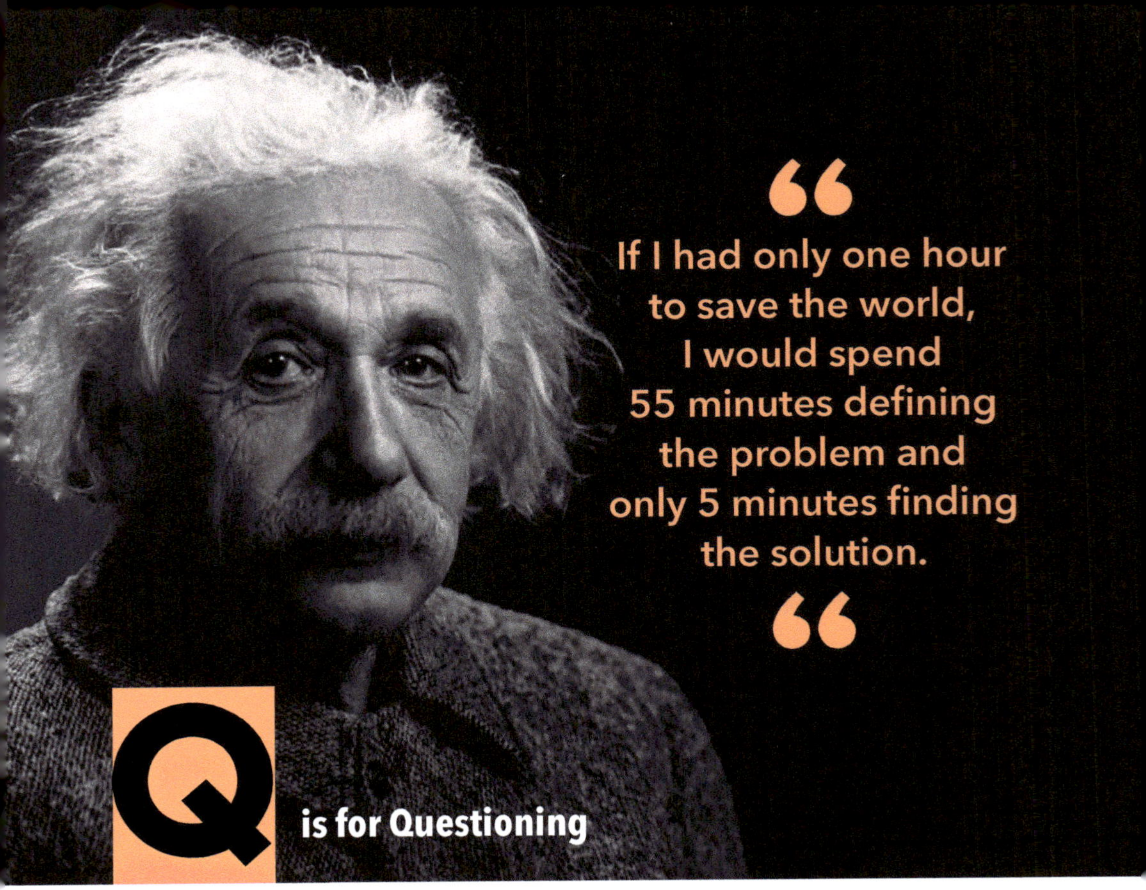

Q is for Questioning

No problem, no opportunity.

We are in the business of solving problems. And "no problem, no opportunity" became a great lens for innovation briefs. If nothing is wrong with current market offers, then it's much more difficult to find successful new iterations. But dig down to find the real consumer problems (whether functional or emotional) and you can then define your innovation brief.

We used the sea squirt story to illustrate this point. Once it is first born and let loose into the ocean, the humble sea squirt has only

one problem in life: to find a rock to make its home. Once this is achieved, it no longer needs a brain – because the brain (as the greatest problem solver ever invented) is now surplus to requirements. So at this point, it actually eats its own brain – and therefore gains nourishment and competitive advantage over other sea squirts!

We would try to interrogate all our client briefs, and look to find the real underlying questions that need to be addressed: the brief behind the brief. Tom's previous company was called 1HQ (and this was also their postcode in Windsor). But they re-purposed the acronym to stand for "one hard question" – the core at the heart of any client brief.

We used question storming techniques, often finding these to be much richer than brain storming. For our clients, our role was often as proactive problem solvers. And if "never stop selling" and "never stop recruiting" became two of our internal drivers, then "never stop questioning" became one of our key client and project drivers.

Q is for Questioning:

- Defining the real problem gives you the best chance of finding new opportunities and successful solutions
- Keep questioning, to find the brief behind the brief
- Question storming techniques can give new and different perspectives

People will forget
what you said.

People will forget
what you did.

**But people will
never forget how you
made them feel**.

Maya Angelou
Author, Poet and Activist

R is for Relationships

Win the person, win the project.

To win new business, the Brand Genetics' principle has always
been "win the person, then win the project." Sometimes the
gap between the two could be as long as five years, but this
does not matter. Building great relationships, and working as
a business partner not just a supplier, is central to achieving
ongoing and sustainable growth – and also enjoyable working
partnerships.

To win the person, you must first understand them as a human
being. Not just their business objectives, but them as a person

too. That means really listening, showing empathy, and finding key points of connection beyond the work. Building a relationship over and beyond the project is not only much more rewarding (for both parties), it's also much better for long-term business building.

I was once asked by a senior client how a particular project was going. My instinctive answer was to talk about the relationships we were building. For example, we had a great session with Ted taking us round the factory, we went out on store checks with Jean from national accounts, and we've got a lunch and stakeholder interview with the marketing head Anne booked for next week. My senior Brand Genetics colleague raised this with me afterwards, saying that her answer would have been all about the project findings to date, and any potential solutions or directions that were emerging. But she noted how the client seemed to be completely satisfied with my different type of answer: it was (at that point) what mattered most to him.

In the early years, as part of our Mutant Marketing Programme, we needed to recruit both Pioneer and Conservative research respondents. We experimented using expensive psychometric tests to find these people. And we brazenly told our clients that we didn't even ask our recruiters to confirm which group was to be with Pioneers, and which with Conservatives; it would be obvious.

We held our first session, researching a new floating spirits innovation – when the spirit sat in a glass above the mixer, like an Irish coffee. The client team were all present in the big group workshop, and we all told ourselves at the end how wonderfully Conservative the respondents had been. But when we called our recruiters the next morning, we found that we had in fact been talking with the psychometrically validated Pioneers! It transpired that people could complete the screening to depict themselves as they wanted to be seen. So we then had the massive challenge of finding a new set of super-extreme Pioneers for the next research session the following week! Fortunately, with a detailed face-to-face briefing, and no psychometric tests in sight, our recruiters delivered in spades, and found us some outstanding new recruits.

We therefore recognised the value of building strong relationships with all our partners, whether they be clients or suppliers. We took a group of about 10 recruiters out for lunch at a restaurant by the river in Hammersmith. None of the recruiters had ever met let alone been entertained by the agencies they worked with before – their role was frequently under-valued and not given the recognition it deserved. This simple initiative helped build some really strong relationships and great loyalty over the coming years. Just as we liked to work with our clients as partners, not suppliers, so it was with our recruiters and local market researchers too. We always looked to build long-term relationships, which built trust and made everything so much easier, more seamless and more enjoyable too.

The moral of the story is, support one another. have empathy and build relationships - because it's in partnership (with peers, partners and clients) that we all get the best results.

R is for Relationships:

- Building great relationships, and working as a business partner not just a supplier, is vital to achieve ongoing and sustainable growth

- Work together and support one another - it's in partnership (with peers, partners and clients) that we all get the best results

- Strive to engage hearts as well as minds, building human relationships above and beyond any project work

S is for Speed

There's no time like the present.

Being a small business, without too much bureaucracy or hierarchy, means you can be responsive and act quickly – and agility has become such a key requirement for big global clients. We pioneered an agile innovation process, and were always rewarded for delivering at speed, and for showing flexibility and adaptability too. We were able to help re-position the world's biggest beer brand, Budweiser, in just six weeks for ABInBev.

Tom and Cliff, who both joined us from Big Green Door, revelled in the autonomy. They had both worked at a brilliant agency, where detail and thoroughness were highly prized. But at Brand Genetics they were able to cut and run, delivering big global projects at real pace. We came to realise that speed and agility were possible when you have less structure and process – and also when you trust and empower your people.

There was one occasion when Michael and Tom pitched for a big project with a major new client in Amsterdam. The presentation went well, but the client also raised some probing questions. Before traveling back to London, Tom and Michael revamped and revised the proposal, and their quick response won us the project. Speed and responsiveness are so important when you're working in the service industry. This is something that has to be drummed into new joiners, who often don't fully appreciate or understand its importance, especially if they're new to the industry.

Alongside speed and agility, there is increasing demand for smartness and succinctness as well. We always used the phrase "everything gets better with editing", inspired by the quote "I would have written you a shorter letter, but I didn't have the time."[34] Clients don't need and can't handle 100-page debriefs these days, so we moved towards 10-page summaries with the detail contained in appendices. We always championed the "debrief on a page" and moved towards a chart in proposals titled "if you only have 60 seconds". We also

---

[34] Sometimes attributed to Oscar Wilde, but more often to Mark Twain or Blaise Pascal

experimented with video and podcast debriefs, and we even put together a debrief drama, played out by actors, to help ABInBev understand what goes on at a house party!

Covid was of course a massive challenge, and the speed at which we were able to adapt was highly impressive. Almost overnight, we had to move seamlessly from face-to-face methodologies to become pioneers in online research, communities and live webinars. We quickly developed new skills, learning to run creative and interactive virtual workshops. Soon we were even delivering online masterclasses, sharing best practice with our clients on how to run engaging remote workshops.

S is for Speed:

- Speed and responsiveness are vital when you're working in the service industry – embrace flexibility and adaptability
- Agility is possible when you have less structure and process – and when you trust and empower your people
- Alongside speed and agility, there is increasing demand for smartness and succinctness as well

is for Team BG

Teamwork makes the dream work!

In business, as in life, people enjoy a sense of belonging. James Kerr's *Legacy*,[35] which gets to the heart of what was once the world's most successful sporting team, New Zealand's legendary All Blacks, sums this up perfectly: "The strength of the wolf is the pack." It's also the human truth that lies at the heart of many successful beer adverts, not least Budweiser's iconic "Wassup" campaign: a celebration of the sense of belonging, so united in this particular tribe that they even communicate with their own non-verbal language.

When we first started Brand Genetics, it was in the days of business cards. Our cards gave each of us a sense of team belonging: we were all unique employees, working under a shared Brand Genetics banner. We even tailored each business card with a unique number, which represented the start date of each individual team member. As we grew, our company name and logo became our unifying badge, which helped us all feel part of the same team with a shared identity.

Over the years, I was often asked by senior clients about working agency side. What were the pros and cons, should they make this move themselves, and how did I gain any job satisfaction when I no longer had direct control over brands or products? The job satisfaction, I explained, came from delivering great work; whether it was adopted or not was up to the client. But it also came from working on and developing our own brand – the Brand Genetics brand. That was something that all the team cared about, and could influence, as key team stakeholders, on an ongoing basis.

I love a team photo. I would always take one at the end of a client workshop, as a celebration with the team of all we had

[35] *Legacy* by James Kerr

achieved together. And team photos were also important mementos of team outings, global work achievements or shared social occasions – whether a team Tough Mudder, a Diwali gathering, a Cardiff half marathon, or company trips to San Sebastián or Lisbon.

We had an office pinboard, which captured some of the great BG moments from across the years, and by including all employees, especially any new joiners, this generated a great sense of team belonging. Another BG tradition became the end-of-year Christmas poem. We always held our Christmas party in January (less crazy with both work and restaurant prices, plus also a nice boost at the start of the New Year). And I would always review the achievements of the previous year in verse – to create a sense of unity and inclusivity, along with humour.

As we found during Covid, a Company is called a Company for a reason – and we all missed the personal togetherness that was challenged by the pandemic. Sure, we could still deliver great work, using new online tools and techniques. But work life is about more than just delivering great work, and teamwork is more than just a series of task-focused transactional Zoom meetings – which is what we were all at times reduced to during the pandemic.

The lockdowns forced us to find new ways to unite as a team – how could we stay together when forced apart? What was the social glue that could hold us all together? And some great initiatives emerged. A Ramadan Relay, when a different team member joined Neha, our Muslim colleague, in fasting with her each day during Ramadan. 15 Minutes of Fame, when a different team member gave a short talk about their own non-work passions (which ranged from beekeeping to novel writing to Bollywood dancing). And a Brand Athletics initiative, when we attempted to log all the team's individual running, walking and cycling kilometres to see if we could collectively get from the UK to Brazil (where our LatAm business is headquartered). In the end, we settled for the Rio Steakhouse in Newcastle instead, and we did manage to make the virtual journey up there from London – and back again! This type of activity was perfect for team bonding – competitive but also collaborative.

Sir Alex Ferguson was a great advocate for a shared team

ethic during his Manchester United days, using a flying geese analogy[36]. Wild geese can travel 70% further when they fly in formation – with a different one taking up the lead at any one time. Sir Alex used this as part of his teamwork philosophy: "Remember the geese", he would say, stopping training and telling his players to look up to the sky, observing the V formation of Canadian geese on their 4,000-mile journey, during which each bird would take its turn at the front.

Sir Alex also always valued the picture of the 11 men who built the Rockefeller Center in Manhattan – precisely because they were one team, united with a common purpose. This picture hung in his office, attracting interest and conversation with everyone from Wayne Rooney to Cristiano Ronaldo.

Teamwork means looking out for one another and having your colleagues' back. I remember being taken to one side halfway through one workshop, when an over-controlling client wanted me to replace my colleague in facilitating a session. I did this, to finish the session in a positive way. But since my highly talented colleague appeared to be too threatening for this particular client – "pearls before swine" – we decided never to work with that client again.

The final word goes back to the All Blacks, who value their team ethic above everything else: "A player who makes the team great is better than a great player."[37] This was never more true than among England's victorious Lionesses, as they won the UEFA Women's Euros at Wembley in 2022.

T is for Team:

- Teamwork is about a shared identity, a sense of belonging, and shared experiences
- Find ways of capturing and celebrating everything that a team has experienced and achieved together
- Teamwork means looking out for one another and having your colleagues' back

---

[36] *Leading* by Sir Alex Ferguson

[37] *Legacy* by James Kerr

U is for Uncertainty

Living with ambiguity.

Working in an ad-hoc project-based consultancy means you must always live with a degree of uncertainty and ambiguity. New business can be a feast or famine experience, and project resourcing becomes a massive and ongoing challenge. How can you ensure your team are all busy enough, but not too busy?

We came to realise that even small businesses need some processes, and these become more important as you grow. The start-up mindset tends to favour intuition and fluidity over structure and systems. Michael always pooh-poohed the idea of a business plan, believing that we would deliver whatever work we could win. I also found the planning process a struggle, relishing the unpredictable and organic challenge of building something from scratch.

But as we grew, we needed to target our new business efforts more purposefully, and systemise many other tasks too. Marc, coming from a more recent client-side background, was always a great cheerleader for process. He introduced and drove our 5-year planning cycle, as well as setting up a highly successful sales and marketing machine. Liz too was great at championing organisation and accountability across the business, and Cat joined the team as an awesomely efficient Head of Finance, which we desperately needed as we grew.

For some reason, a lot of the great systems we found began with H! There was Harvest for managing resourcing, Hubspot for tracking all our new business leads and project work, and HiBob for all our HR initiatives. We also found a brilliant subscription service, Vestd, to manage all our share transactions, legal documentation and agreements. These systems all helped us manage the business better, allowing us to work smarter, not harder.

Another challenge was to structure for sustainable and human-first growth. As we grew, we needed to get more disciplined in defining people's roles and responsibilities, empowering them with the autonomy to make decisions within their own remit. We tried to define how each person's contribution input and built to our overall vision. We were inspired in this by the story of John F Kennedy touring NASA headquarters in 1962, and asking a janitor who was sweeping the floor, "What are you doing?" The reply came back, "Mr President, I'm helping put a man on the moon."

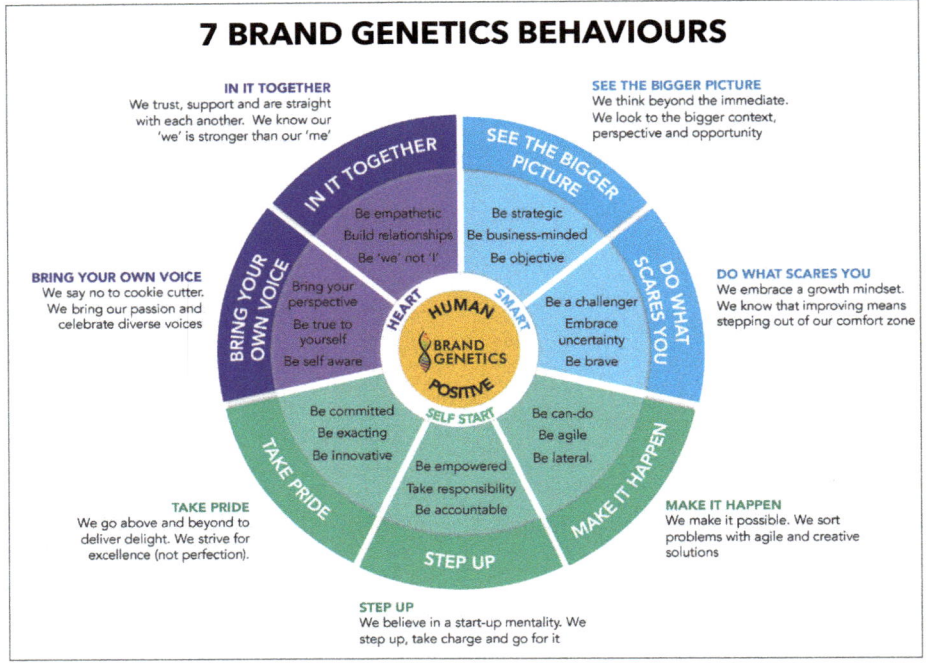

Fiona and Frankie pioneered and authored a great set of BG Behaviours, which helped set out what we expected from BG people – both the current team, but also future hires. These were grouped into a Smart category (See the Bigger Picture and Do What Scares You), a Heart one (In It Together and Bring Your Own Voice) plus also a Self-Start set of behaviours (Step Up, Make It Happen and Take Pride). This became a useful lens to look through both during performance reviews, and also for questioning during the recruitment process. Simon took this further, producing themed updates to celebrate achievements against the key behaviours, and instigating company awards for stand-out examples.

Mia and Frankie worked to develop a set of BG Capabilities, which articulated what traits BG people needed to learn and master in order to succeed and progress. If the Behaviours were about 'being', the Capabilities were about 'doing'. This all took time, both to initiate and then to embed across the business. But it helped drive understanding and expectations, removing doubt and uncertainty.

But whatever systems we put in place, we realised that our people still had to be comfortable living with ambiguity. The nature of an ad-hoc consultancy business dictates this. Workloads are constantly changing, and they're often challenging too. Some people rise to this challenge, embracing the excitement of ever-changing briefs and projects. But others need more structure and certainty. Fortunately, not many of our hires failed. But one who did struggle was a very bright and talented individual for whom our dynamic and unpredictable environment was just ill suited.

Fortunately, both sides recognised this, and she went on to excel elsewhere, in a more predictable and structured business.

We also had to challenge our clients on occasions, and force them to live with ambiguity too. Future-focused work, when you're trying to invent the future, is not always a clear, linear or straightforward process. I always liked this diagram about what constitutes success, and I often used it with clients when we were midway through a challenging project.

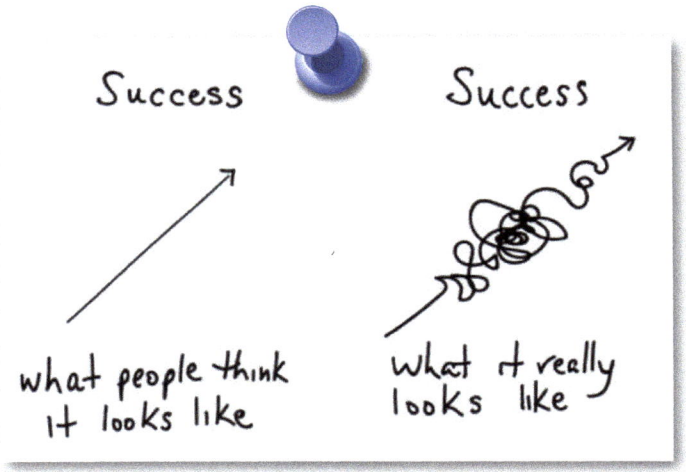

Covid of course drove massive uncertainty across the industry and indeed the world. But it also helped us to experiment more, and learn new skills. Even now, the new reality of hybrid working comes with a degree of uncertainty. But as so often, we found the best route through was to try things out, to 'test and learn'. Only then can uncertainty give way to things that carry a little more certainty!

U is for Uncertainty:

- Recognise the difference between the start-up mindset of intuition and fluidity, and the scale-up one that needs more structure and process

- Empower people to make their own decisions, by clearly defining roles and responsibilities, and setting out expectations, behaviours and required capabilities

- But recognise that you will always have to live with a degree of ambiguity and uncertainty

is for Values

Values are like lighthouses; they are signals giving us direction, meaning and purpose.[38]

Shared values are central to any relationship, and any business relationship is no different. When I first joined Michael and John at the start of our Brand Genetics journey, Michael had recently moved on from a previous agency, where he had worked with his co-owner and business partner for well over 10 years. "Think of it as a marriage," Michael advised, "but rather more important!" I came to appreciate what he meant. Shared values are vital between founders and business owners, and between employees as the team grows too. And this isn't always easy. In the end, when we parted company

with John, and when Michael subsequently left to retire, then if not full-blown messy divorces, these were both certainly very difficult, taxing and energy-sapping experiences.

As we grew, we liked to talk about what it meant to be a 'BG-er'. But this existed mainly in our own minds, and it was difficult to articulate or share with other people. How could we define the shared value set or 'glue' that helped make Brand Genetics unique, and held the team and business together? If we could 'bottle' this, it would be a great definition of our culture, and an invaluable aid to help new joiners understand and integrate too.

I therefore worked with Cliff to develop a 5-point company

38 Recruiter Journal: www.wow4u.com

Manifesto, covering the key principles which governed how Brand Genetics works. This proved to be a great calling card for us, and became visible across the business – on walls, on mugs and even in the toilet! It helped us identify when things were going well, but also when they were not. Because, to quote Bill Bernbach,[39] "A principle isn't a principle until it costs you something." So our value set helped us manage some difficult people situations on a couple of occasions, because it was an objective measure of when (for example) people were not being collaborative or acting in the best interests of the team.

BRAND GENETICS

MANIFESTO

These 5 principles govern the way Brand Genetics works...

Be uniquely human

We believe the best teams are made from diverse personalities and perspectives working together. So be yourself, recognise and celebrate your unique strengths and talents (as well as those of others) and say 'no' to the cookie cutter!

What makes you special is what makes us special

Embrace being 'comfortably uncomfortable'

Nurture your interest in the new and different, explore the unusual and the adjacent. Breaking new ground is a journey of learning – it keeps us fresh, but it's challenging. There are times you'll fail: embrace it – real learning never comes without it.

Don't settle for the status quo – stay curious, remain restless

Keep calm and collaborate

The BG 'we' means we always operate as a team, winning together and overcoming challenges together. Support one another, have empathy and build relationships, as it's in partnership (with peers, partners & clients) that we get the best results.

Teamwork makes the dream work!

Fun isn't just for Feelgood Friday

We know laughing increases creativity, reduces stress, and teams that laugh together achieve more. What we do isn't brain surgery, so enjoy it, help others enjoy it and celebrate the successes, big and small – no one's ever died from a broken workshop...

You don't have to be serious to solve serious issues

Make time for yourself

While we care about what we do, and always go the extra mile to deliver delight, we need to care about ourselves too. So lunch is lunch, holidays are holidays, and taking time to switch off will make you more productive, more creative and happier too!

You can't do a great job if your job is all you do

---

[39] Bill Bernbach, US Advertising Creative Director

Monica was a great addition to Brand Genetics. She arrived from Brazil, where she had held senior client-side jobs at Unilever. She wanted to work with us for three months one summer, before doing a Masters course in Spain. But she changed her mind after her first week with us. She said she felt that BG was more like a home than an office, and the team were more like family than colleagues. She said she didn't want to put any pressure on us, but she was pulling out of her planned Masters. Monica joined us full-time and was an instant success.

But her story is interesting, because it also caused us to question what role we play in people's lives. I have heard of other people who have left start-ups to join more conventional and established businesses, and found it to be a much less rich or fulfilling experience. The advantage can be that your job is just your job – you can do it, go home and forget about it. But your work relationships are then just transactional – and a job should (ideally) be about more than just that.

Tom rightly challenged the assertion that we were a 'family' – on the basis that you can never leave a family, and they can be highly dysfunctional too! Fiona neatly squared this circle, saying we embraced family values, without actually being one. Our role as a business should be to value our people, to understand them as fully as possible, and to be wholly supportive of them too. But we should also treat our people as adults, recognising that they can sort out their own lives for themselves – so we're not their family.

When this works, great things can happen. I remember one occasion when internal career progression enabled a team member to turn down an external offer, saying "thank you for giving me the opportunity to continue to do the job I love." Both work and life too should surely be about doing the things we love, alongside people with a shared value set.

V is for Values:

- Shared values help define a company, and can unite founders and team members alike

- Defining your core company values and giving them visibility will help bring the team together

- A job should ideally be about more than just the work – it is doing what we love, alongside people with a shared value set

W

is for We

Keep calm and collaborate.

Together we are stronger, so we always talk about the "BG we." This book is certainly not about the "AC me." Our motto is "Keep calm and collaborate." Every project has a team of at least two people, and can always draw on the wider wisdom of the extended BG mindset as well. We win together, and face challenges together too.

Ben became a great Brand Genetics advocate with a real talent for new business. But I remember a conversation with him when he first joined us as a student intern. He sent an email to a client saying "I believe..." While I admired his confidence, I explained to him that "We believe" would be a much stronger approach. He should use the power of the collective, or the "BG we." Ben learnt quickly, so never had to be told again.

No one person has all the wisdom or all the answers, so it is never a problem to ask for help. The boy in Charlie Mackesy's story realises this, when he asks the horse, what's the bravest thing you've ever said?[40] Mackesy also says that "Asking for help isn't giving up... It's refusing to give up."

---

[40] *The Boy, The Mole, The Fox and The Horse* © Charlie Mackesy

We used the diversity of the BG team – marketers, psychologists, researchers, strategists, entrepreneurs – to make for a much stronger 'we'.

In the very early days, we were a team of just three people. What united us was a shared endeavour. It was as if the three of us were all in a small rowing boat together, maybe it was even called Shared Endeavour, and there were several times when we nearly capsized. But if you're all rowing in the same direction, and shouldering the same burden, then everything becomes possible and achievable. And the contrary is also true. As soon as John decided he wanted to pursue other activities outside of Brand Genetics, that destroyed the common bond or shared endeavour. So that became the first major storm we had to face up to.

> **W is for We:**
>
> - Together we are stronger: face challenges together, and win together
> - It is never a problem to ask for help – use the wisdom and diversity of the collective 'we'
> - Finding and maintaining a shared endeavour is central for success

is for X-Factor

Defining your USP: finding your secret sauce.

What makes a company unique? How are you special and different? Defining our own "secret sauce" was critical to our success. It's often not an easy or straightforward process, but it's vital to articulate a clear definition of your business USP (unique selling point). Not every client needs it spelt out on every occasion. But (as with the purchase decision behind so many consumer packaged goods) it's the rational reason to justify and underpin what can sometimes be an emotional choice.

Paul was always pushing and challenging our thinking on this, questioning what did Brand Genetics really stand for? Michael was also a keen advocate of 'praxis', which he defined as the practical application of academic theory and thinking. He even used to joke about some of our work, saying "that's all very well in practice, but what's the theory?!"

John pioneered the Mutant Marketing Programme, and encouraged us to look at consumer markets through "gene goggles" – what insights and understanding could we gain from evolutionary science? Paul took up this theme, saying that the modern consumer mind was "more suited to the savannah than the supermarket," and for a while we looked at markets through the 3 x S's of our evolutionary heritage: sex, status and survival.

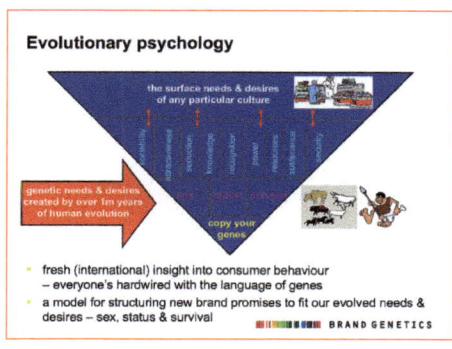

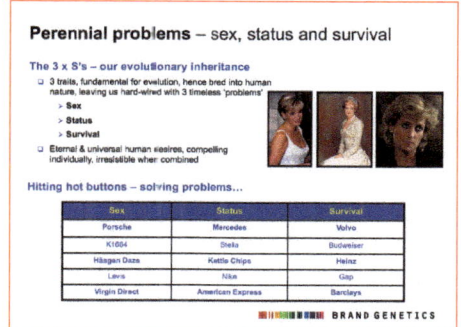

So we were grounded in consumer psychology and human sciences from the start, and this gave us a solid foundation and framework for our work. Cliff's psychology and Liz's behavioural science backgrounds helped us sharpen this thinking, and we were able to articulate four distinct lenses to help support our human-first positioning:

- Human Sciences – leveraging psychology and behavioural economics to provide deeper insight, and to ground our findings in evidence

- Human Empathy – using immersive ways to help see the world through the eyes of the consumer, to understand deeper emotional connections

- Human Behaviour – using varied data sources to observe and understand real-life behaviour and decisions, to uncover the unseen and unspoken

- Human Futures – looking to the edges and drawing on divergent perspectives to offer foresight, to help understand the direction of change

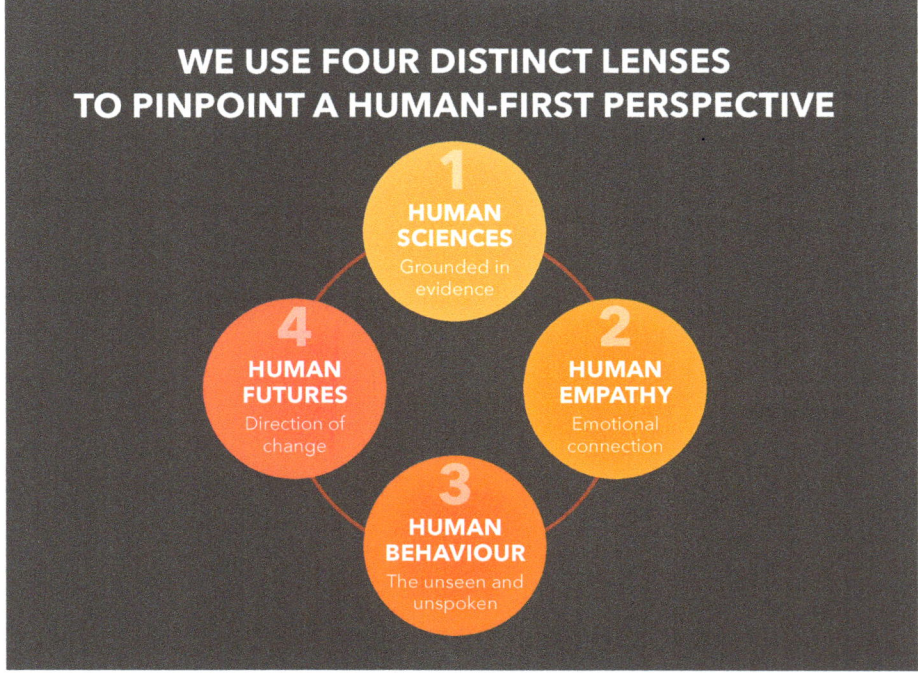

This focus and approach helped us to understand human beings and their purchasing behaviour – to get to the real "job to be done." These tools and techniques allowed us to unlock what people don't, won't or can't articulate logically themselves. The combination ensured we could access those deep-rooted human truths that unite humanity, as opposed to those that divide it.

This became our X-Factor, giving us the building blocks to identify positive growth for our clients. And we helped develop internal knowledge and skillsets by setting up the BG Academy, featuring all the latest learning delivered by our resident consumer psychologist, Dr Paul

X is for X-Factor:

- Understand your company's USP, and define what makes you special and different
- You must be able to articulate the rational reason behind an emotional choice
- It is then important to upskill and train the team to help deliver this

Y is for You

What makes you special is what makes us special.

We believed in people being uniquely themselves. Not putting on a work self, but feeling free to be the same person at work as out of work.

I found this out from personal experience. When I worked in client-side marketing roles, I soon realised that marketers in big corporate companies are also very skilled at marketing themselves. Sometimes, it was more important "to be seen to be doing a good job" than actually to be doing one! I found out that I was able to put on the corporate suit and play this game, but it was increasingly at cost of me being my true self.

So when we set up Brand Genetics, I was conscious that there can be a work self to people, and also a true self. I wanted these to come together, but not just in the middle. I wanted people to be able to be their true selves at Brand Genetics – warts and all! Cliff in particular embraced this mindset in the early days. He would (and could) come to work in his T-shirt, shorts and sandals, and latterly with his dog Finn as well. That was Cliff's true self – and we loved him for it. He didn't have to compromise this in any way.

We wanted to celebrate people's unique strengths, not beat them up for their weaknesses. We encouraged all our people "to be uniquely human," and took the view that what makes them distinctive and individual is what could help make us distinctive and individual too. We therefore relished and enjoyed people's diversity and individuality, and discouraged a conformist mindset.

There is sometimes a false perception that "the business" is an entity with a mind of its own. But a business is nothing more than the collection of people who inhabit it at any one time. If you drew a line around everyone who was part of Brand Genetics at any given time, that was "the business". Our skillsets were the skillsets of the individual people, and our voice and culture were defined by these same people too.

We therefore tried to look for people from a 'culture add' perspective as opposed to a straight 'culture fit'. A business culture must be given the freedom to adapt and evolve. And the divergent opinions of individual team members can only energise and inspire, helping us to see the world differently and prompt new thinking. It was a powerful and empowering way to treat our people, and it enabled us to harness and leverage people's unique and individual talents. I guess the clue is in the name, Brand Genetics. The freedom for unique human DNA's to thrive, all under a collective company banner.

Y is for You:

- Allow people to be their unique selves – not a work self, but a true self
- Celebrate people's unique strengths, don't beat them up for their weaknesses
- A business is defined by the collection of people who inhabit it at any one time – so ensure you harness and leverage everyone's unique and individual talents

Z is for Zero to One

On the origin of species.

We often talk about the "zero to one" of innovation. How do you start something from nothing, when you just have a blank piece of paper? Once you have an initial idea, then it can be built and evolved. One can go to two, two to five, five to 10 and 10 to 100. Every subsequent innovation or iteration is an incremental step. Once you stand for something, everything else becomes "descent with modification", to use Darwinian language. But true and genuine invention, that first step from zero to one, is infinite. When the original Macintosh team invented the smart phone, they say there was no "standing on

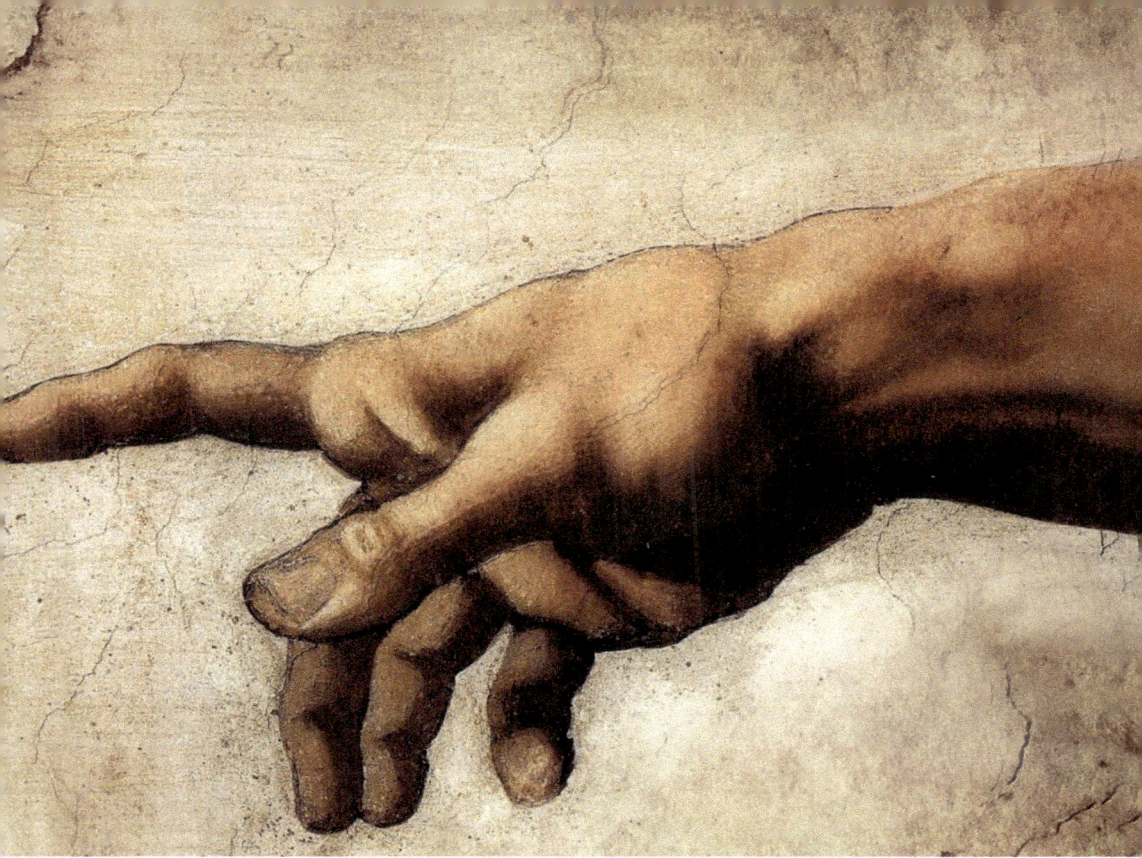

the shoulders of giants;"[41] instead, they had to build the giant from the toes upwards.[42]

The same is true for starting a new business. Brand Genetics' first ever paper boldly proclaimed, "All Marketing is Darwinian." John wrote this thesis, one of his original and entertaining rants, selling the virtues of blind variation and selective retention. If Darwin studied the evolution of the beaks of finches on the Galápagos Islands, with natural selection giving competitive advantage to certain variations, then surely we could use a similar model for new brand innovation? The only thing we would advocate in addition

---

[41] Isaac Newton and others

[42] Marc Porat and Sarah Kerruish: *General Magic Movie*

was speed to market: our clients wouldn't want to wait several million years!

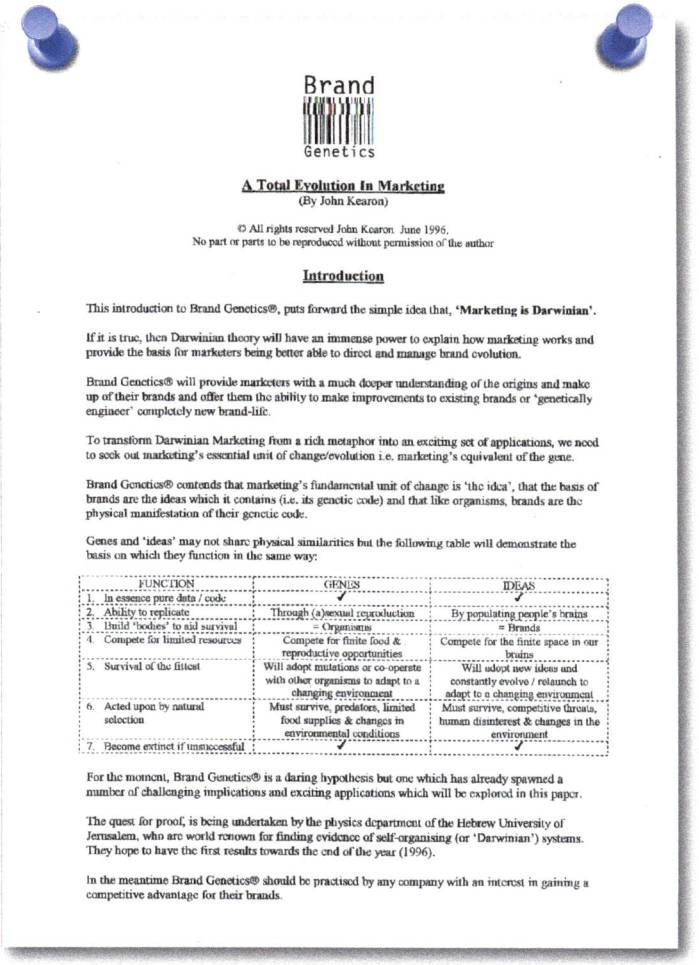

We first registered the company as Mutant Marketing Limited, but fortunately sanity prevailed, and we changed our name to Brand Genetics after our first 18 months. The name was strong and distinctive, even if it was sometimes misunderstood or misinterpreted over the years. We were occasionally misspelt as "Brand Generics" (the antithesis of what we were trying to stand for); we were once mutated phonetically into "Brands in Essex"; and we were regally introduced onto a Russian research conference platform in Moscow as "Grand Genetics"!

The start-up days were spent working between our three respective homes: Murray Mews in Camden where Michael lived, Hampton in South-West London which was my home, and notably The Ark, the room above John's garage in St Albans, which became our war room. We stayed true to our Darwinian principles – even presenting our first ever client with a 'Darwin' award (akin to an Oscar) for creating new brand life via the first ever BG launch. It was Winalot Fish Favourites, which were treats for dogs, launched by Jonathan from Spillers Petfoods.

For any new idea, and indeed for any business, I think it's important to know about the roots, origins and history. When I was client-side, I always found it insightful and informative to ask a creative where he or she got their idea from, when they were presenting a new advertising campaign. It massively helps your understanding. So we always inducted new joiners with a short history of Brand Genetics. And now it has been possible to write up this slightly longer history, to reflect on all we've done and achieved over 25 years, sharing some of the learning and the journey to date.

My Brand Genetics experience has been a 25-year rollercoaster. I have worked with brilliant people, and we have run some amazing projects. We helped our clients create some highly successful new products, such as Robinsons Fruit Shoot, Cadbury's Little Treasures, Stella Artois Unfiltered and Budweiser brewed with 100% renewable energy. Maybe the best idea that was never launched was a range of Single Island Rums for Bacardi. And the worst? It's probably a toss-up between Ovaltine Sticking Plasters and Friskies Sticky Meals (described as "luminous gel you stick to trees, walls or the ceiling; time-sensitive, it slowly slides down, driving your dog crazy with anticipation!"). To quote Charles Dickens, "It was the best of times, it was the worst of times; it was the age of wisdom, it was the age of foolishness."[43]

I sign off with massive pride for all that Brand Genetics has done, built and achieved, both past, present and future. I feel privileged and humbled to have worked with so many exceptional people over the years – not just great professionals, but more importantly great human beings. Many thanks to you all, and I truly hope that Brand Genetics is still surviving, thriving and evolving in 25 years' time. All in the best traditions of evolution!

---

[43] Charles Dickens, *A Tale of Two Cities*

Z is for Zero to One:

- Starting up is an act of true and genuine invention – everything else is incremental

- A new start-up needs to embrace naivety, alongside self-belief

- Any new idea, and indeed any new business, is defined by its the roots, origins and history – so interrogate and understand these

PICTURE CREDITS

Page 14   © Cliff Fawcett

Page 16   rigsbyphoto/Shutterstock.com

Page 17   © Edward Monkton

Page 18   Noddy/abebooks.com

Page 22   Daniel Gale/Shutterstock.com

Page 30   Grindstone Media Group/Shutterstock.com

Page 38   Good to Great/Rickkettner.com

Page 50   Happy Nati/Shutterstock.com

Page 54   Andrewshots/Shutterstock.com

Page 56   © Charlie Mackesy

Page 60   Banksy Letting Love Go! Balloon Girl! by ThatMerchStore and
             background setting by Samantha Gades @unsplash

Page 72   graphicwithart/Shutterstock.com

Page 86   (top image) Einstein/in the public domain

Page 86   (bottom image) Ogurtsov/Shutterstock.com

Page 88   John David Mercer/AP

Page 92   © Cliff Fawcett

Page 100   Lunch atop a Skyscraper 1932 © Corbis Images

Page 102   dotini/Shutterstock.com

Page 106   Attributed to Demetri Martin, author of *This Is A Book*

Page 108   Kevin Eaves/Shutterstock.com

Page 115   © Charlie Mackesy

Page 118   Secret Sauce @Cathy Heng

Page 126   Printexstar/Shutterstock.com

WITH THANKS

With many thanks to those who have
read and commented on early drafts, and for
their encouragement and advice –
family members Helen, Mia and Rachel,
colleagues Paul, Cliff and Tom,
and friends Andy and Nick.

With heartfelt thanks to Cathy[44] for
both the cover design and the internal art direction –
you have brought everything to life so beautifully!

With massive thanks to Hannah[45] from Matador
for your efficiency and expertise
on taking me through the publishing process.

---

[44] Cathy Heng: www.cathyheng.com
[45] Hannah Dakin: www.troubador.co.uk